TALES OF CONFLICT

by B.A. McKelvie

Inside front cover and chapter
illustrations by C.P. Connorton.

A Cowichan warrior. The braves from
the four villages in the Cowichan Valley
were especially notorious, preying on
both Indians and whites. (See page 72.)

THE COVERS

FRONT: Nootka Sound, where in 1803 all but two of the *Boston's* crew were massacred.

INSIDE FRONT: A painting by C.P. Connorton of Chief Alexis galloping to meet Govenor Seymour. Had Chief Alexis not remained neutral in the war, casualties would have been far higher.

INSIDE BACK: The policy of the fur traders was to leave the Indians alone as long as they confined murders and massacres to each other. The painting is reproduced courtesy The Royal Ontario Museum, Toronto, Canada.

OUTSIDE BACK: In the Fraser Canyon in 1858 upwards of 200 Indians and miners were killed in the province's most bloody Indian-white conflict.

PHOTO CREDITS

B.C. Provincial Archives, front and back covers, 8, 9, 18-19, 24, 26, 27, 33, 38-39, 42, 46, 50, 54, 58, 59, 61, 66, 67, 76, 80, 81, 85, 86, 91, 94, 98, 99, 104-105, 110-111; Curtis, E.P., 1, 81, 124, 125; Geological Survey of Canada, 41; Glenbow-Alberta Institute, 110, 113; Heritage House, inside front cover, 90, 114; Imperial Oil, 14; Parks Canada, Map, 38; Provincial Archives of Alberta, 113; Public Archives of Canada, 32-33, 41; Royal Ontario Museum, inside back cover; Tourism B.C., front and back covers; Vancouver City Archives, 70; *Vancouver Province,* inside back cover; Vancouver Public Library, 50, 74-75, 85, 90, 124, 125.

CANADIAN CATALOGUING IN PUBLICATION DATA

McKelvie, B.A. (Bruce Alistair), 1889-1960.
    Tales of Conflict

Reprint. Originally published:
Vancouver: Vancouver Daily Province, 1949.

ISBN 0-919214-66-5

1. Northwest, Canadian - History - To 1870.* 2. British Columbia - History - 1849-1871.* 3. Indians of North America - British Columbia - History. I. Title.
FC3822.M394 1985   971.1'02   C85-091053-6
F1088.M394 1985

HERITAGE HOUSE
PUBLISHING COMPANY LTD.
Box 1228, Station A
Surrey, B.C. V3S 2B3

Printed in Canada

CONTENTS

ACKNOWLEDGMENT
Tales of Conflict was originally published in 1950 by the *Vancouver Daily Province*. Heritage House thanks The Southam Newspaper Group for permission to reprint.
    The articles in *Tales of Conflict* are timeless and illustrate to new generations that B.C.'s formative years were not dull but vibrant, although at times both bloody and tragic.

THE AUTHOR:
Bruce A. McKelvie, 1890-1960, was one of B.C.'s foremost historians. He was born in Vancouver when the city had a population of 8,000 and used to hunt grouse where Vancouver's city hall now stands.
    He became a newspaperman, his career spanning half a century and making him probably B.C.'s best known political and police reporter. During his career he worked on many newspapers, including the *Vancouver Province* and the *Daily Colonist* in Victoria where he was managing editor for seven years. He waged many campaigns to preserve B.C.'s rich heritage. For instance, Petroglyph Park near Nanaimo, the site of prehistoric Indian paintings, was established because of his interest.

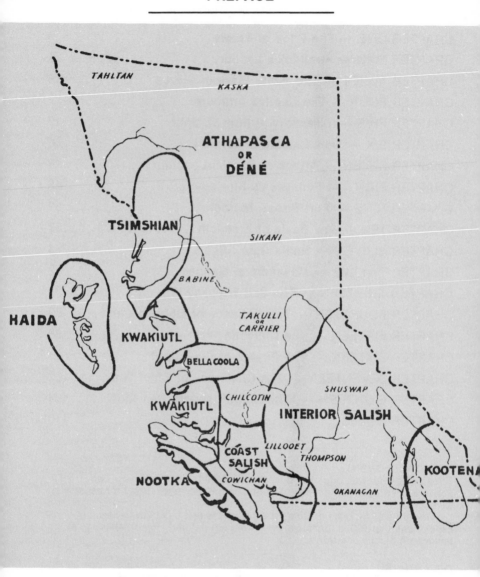

Language boundaries of the Indians when the white men arrived.

Few people realize how many tragic happenings marked the earlier years of provincial settlement. The problem was not to find events of which to write, but to select those that were representative and could be authenticated. There are many exciting episodes in which the records are less explicit, and still others, of which there can be no doubt, but which are lacking in detail. Among these latter, is the story told by Dr. J.S. Helmcken of the manner in which he and J.W. McKay, and the forces they led, were defeated in an attempt to arrest some Indians at the Songhee's village.

There were many such differences, as well as more serious affrays with the Indians in and about Fort Victoria. In fact a large book might be written about them. There was the attack made by the natives on the Hudson's Bay Company's farm at Cadboro Bay, when Bailey, the bailiff of the place, was knocked on the head, and Governor James Douglas led a mounted group at a gallop over the bush trail to the rescue. Then there was the affair of the *Royal Charlie,* when a schooner of that name was fired upon from the Indian encampment on the harbor, and naval forces had to be secured in order to arrest the guilty men. At Nanaimo, upon one occasion, residents had to gather at the Bastion for protection when the carronades were fired over the Haida camp to make those fierce warriors surrender a member of the tribe who was wanted for some misdemeanor. There were several occasions when Fort Kamloops was in peril, and once it had to be abandoned when the officer in charge, Samuel Black, was murdered, but these stories have been told, and very ably, by the late Dr. Mark Wade and by other capable writers.

The Indians were a remarkable people, with their own fixed laws, social and commercial organizations and cultural and artistic standards. The fact that in little more than half a century they had progressed from savagery to citizenship indicates their adaptability and progress. The stories related here deal with those earlier years before their acceptance of the white man's civilization had advanced sufficiently to win for them the full responsibilities entailed by the franchise.

Every endeavor has been made to obtain facts in respect of the incidents included in this book. Official records, despatches, letters of proceedings of naval operations, log books and contemporary newspapers have been consulted. Much information has been obtained that is new to the present day public, such as the massacre on board the Boston schooner *Resolution* at Cumshewa Inlet in 1794 and details of the treacherous attack on Guy Hughes and others at Fort St. John in 1823. The story of what happened on the Peace River and at Fort George in that year, and in 1828 at Fraser Lake has been obtained through the kindness of the Governor and Committee of the Hudson's Bay Company, London. . . .

The publication of this volume is a further evidence of the great contribution being made by the *Vancouver Daily Province* to the preservation, in permanent form, of the colorful story of British Columbia.

B.A. McKelvie
Cobble Hill, B.C.

CHAPTER ONE

The Price of Safety

Traders along the B.C. coast in the early 1800s were often so concerned with sea otter skins that they overlooked their own safety. As a consequence, many sailors were killed, including the entire crew of the trading vessel *Tonquin*.

Contrary to popular belief, the conquest of the great territory west of the Rocky Mountains and north of the 49th parallel by the white men was not an easy task. The Indians resisted. They did so with bravery and cunning. At times their audacity tested all the powers of local authority.

There were bound to be clashes. The Indian, following his age-old traditions and enjoying his own ways of life, knew nothing of these strangers. The European trader, having only a hazy idea of the multitudinous laws of his kind, was equally ignorant of the customs of the native, but assumed that he was a superior being and consequently held the red man in contempt.

The Indians who inhabited what is now British Columbia were fierce fighters. They were treacherous in attack and ruthless in avenging a real or imagined wrong. They were extremely proud and sensitive. Their lives were measured by intricate rules and the protocols of a complex social organization, and by their superstitious fears.

Too many early navigators were concerned only with securing full cargoes of sea otter skins. They had neither time nor inclination to study the niceties of procedure in dealing with savages. And frequently they forgot that vigilance was the price of safety.

The Indians, of the coast particularly, were piratical by instinct. Their mode of life as well as the inclination that they may have inherited from Mongolian ancestors ruled out any other system.

Enmity was not necessarily personal. Retaliation by sudden attack from ambush was made upon inoffensive members of the family or tribe of any enemy. Overt acts were not required to justify atrocious attacks — jealousy or covetousness sufficed, and often started feuds or caused butchery. When the traders' ships came laden with things to dazzle the mind and capture the fancy of the Indian, it would have been a miracle if the tribesmen did not conspire to take these treasures at such a slight cost as a piratical attack. The maritime merchants did not stay long enough at any one locality to master the language. They invented a jargon that would serve the minimum requirements of barter. The natives became proficient in the use of the limited vocabulary, but they learned very little about the white visitors who came in such big canoes. Even the nationalities of the ships and the people with whom they dealt were confusing to the natives. They called all who hailed from British lands "King George Men," while those who came under the Star Spangled Banner of United States were — and are to this day — "Boston Men."

The Indians of the west coast of Vancouver's Island (as Vancouver Island was originally named) were better acquainted with the traders than were any others. But there, too, they would not hesitate to take treacherous advantage of the whites if vigilance were relaxed. There are several outstanding examples of Indians seizing an opportunity of attacking a vessel when too great a trust was placed in the seemingly peaceful war chiefs. In one instance no justification whatever was given for the massacre of a number of whites. In the other case, however, there was a motive, according to the blood code of the Indians.

The first of these attacks was made on the Boston ship *Atahualpa* in Spiller Passage, Milbanke Sound, in June 1805; the other, the capture of John Jacob Astor's fine vessel, the *Tonquin,* in Clayoquot Sound in 1811, with the loss of every white member of the crew.

The *Atahualpa* was a fine craft. She had been anchored off an Indian village where Chief Kaiete lived with a host of savage warriors. For several days trading went on harmoniously between Captain Oliver Porter and the natives. There was no apparent cause for suspicion, and as a result no special precautions were taken against a surprise attack.

It was on the morning of June 13, 1805. The captain was bending over the rail, inspecting a pelt that an Indian in a canoe was holding up. Large numbers of natives had been quietly gathering about the *Atahualpa,* and those from several big canoes had been permitted to board the ship. They scattered over the deck. A war chief approached Captain Porter. There was nothing unusual noticed in his movements until suddenly he picked up a trade coat and threw it over the head of the officer. Then whipping out a dagger from beneath his mantle he plunged it into the white man's back and threw him overboard.

Instantly the Indians on deck produced knives and attacked the surprised sailors. Chief Mate John Hill was badly wounded, but managed to throw himself down into the cabin where he secured firearms. He returned to the deck to commence firing at the yelling savages as they chased other white men about the ship. John Goodman, second mate, fell mortally wounded in the first assault; John G. Rickstraw, another officer, also went down under the death-dealing daggers of the Indian killers. Lyman Plummer, nephew of the ship's owner, was badly wounded but lived long enough to help in directing the eventual escape of the survivors. Isaac Summers, cooper; Luther Lapman, Samuel Lapman and Peter Spooner, seamen; and John Williams, cook, were killed. Williams fought with amazing bravery, and as long as his supply of boiling water in the galley lasted, he beat off all efforts to reach him. He scalded a number of the pirates before they cut him down. Three seamen, a

The Coastal Indians' cedar canoes, above, were massive. In them they raided each other's territory, murdering and taking slaves.

This drawing is believed to be the only detailed one of the *Tonquin,* a large, well armed vessel attacked by Indians in Clayoquot Sound in June 1811. All but one of her crew were massacred. The survivor died later, but not before exacting a terrible revenge.

Sandwich Islander (Hawaiian) and a Kodiac (Kodiak) Indian were seriously wounded, while five men were slightly injured. Only three sailors and a Sandwich Islander escaped without hurt.

Several others managed to follow Hill's example and reach the cabin and obtain firearms. By the rapidity of their fire they finally drove the Indians from the deck. But the savages were not yet defeated. They were unwilling to give up a prize that had already cost them a number of casualties. A great war canoe, crowded with men, attacked the bow cable, attempting to cut it, so the vessel would swing round and ground. This manoeuvre was detected. A swivel was loaded with grape shot and was trained upon them. From a distance of only a few feet it was fired. The effect was terrible. The cedar dug-out burst into a thousand pieces, while mangled and dying warriors were tossed over a wide area. One wounded Indian alone reached shore. There were more than twenty in the canoe.

At least that many more died in the fight on board the ship. On the *Atahualpa,* Captain Porter and nine of his men were dead, nine more were wounded and only four escaped.

After firing a few shots at the village, the survivors managed to shake out sufficient sails to get the ship under way and she headed across the Sound in search of other trading vessels to obtain help for the wounded and additional men to man the vessel.

Even Indian tradition does not suggest that there was any cause other than piracy for the attack on the *Atahualpa.* It was different in the matter of the *Tonquin.* Captain Jonathan Thorn had, himself, insulted an Indian chief, and had resolutely refused to adopt the suggestion of Alexander McKay, the experienced Indian trader, that the ship quit the locality.

Jonathan Thorn was a lieutenant in the United States navy, one of the heroes of the Republic's war with Tripoli. As a naval officer he was, no doubt, efficient, but in command of an expedition to trade trinket for furs he was out of place. He possessed a quick and active temper and was a strict disciplinarian whose straightforward nature could not tolerate the bickering and bargaining in which the Indians delighted.

In June 1811, the *Tonquin* left the newly established trading post of Astoria, on the Columbia River, for a trip to the north in search of sea otter skins. A few days later she dropped anchor in Clayoquot Sound. Tradition says that it was June 15 that Thorn quarrelled with Chief Nookamis. He became irritated at the actions of the Indian haggling over the sale of a pelt, and, seizing the fur from the chief's hands, rubbed it over his face. Here was a real insult, that to an Indian could only be wiped out in blood.

McKay, the Indian trader, advised the captain to up anchor and sail away. He knew the deadly nature of the insult. Captain Thorn, however, was in no temper to accept advice, nor would he authorize extra precautions against attack. He was confident that he could, backed by a white crew, defend the well armed *Tonquin* against any force of Indians.

Next morning the natives came out in large numbers. They offered their best furs at reasonable prices — for knives. They seemed to be in a festive mood, and none more so than Nookamis. He, with a young war chief, Shewish, and some fighting men boarded the ship. The captain was in his cabin when Shewish gave the signal. Knives flashed as the attack began. James Lewis was the first casualty. He was wounded but managed to escape to the rigging. He was the last to die, and when he did he exacted an awful revenge upon his assailants.

Captain Thorn, hearing the war-whoops and scuffling on deck, rushed up the companionway without stopping to arm himself. As he emerged Chief Shewish sprang at him. Thorn only had time to open his clasp knife, and this he plunged into the skull of the Indian, killing him. An instant later he, himself, fell, with a number of daggers in his vitals.

One by one officers and men fell. At last the wounded Lewis and four others who had joined him in the rigging alone remained alive of the ship's company. They managed to slide down a stay and enter the cabin through a port. Now they obtained arms, and breaking a hole through the companionway side were able to open fire on the deck. So hotly did they maintain this fire that the Indians retreated to the shore.

Lewis wanted the men to try and work the vessel away from Clayoquot. They feared their inability to do so, and determined to quit the ship that night in a small boat. Lewis refused to join them, so they left him. They were later captured and brought back to be tortured to death.

The wounded man made careful and deliberate preparations on board the *Tonquin* during the hours of darkness. When daylight came again, he appeared on deck and beckoned for the Indians to come and pillage the vessel. They were only too agreeable. They swarmed out and soon were all over the vessel. They could not find Lewis, but that did not matter. He could not escape, and there were so many treasures for them to have for the taking.

Suddenly there was a hissing sound. Then with a deafening explosion and blinding flash, the ship burst asunder. Lewis had avenged his companions. He had fired the powder magazine.

The Indian interpreter alone survived the massacre. From the story that he later told the tale was pieced together. But there was another witness, who years later, partially at least, corroborated the testimony of the interpreter. He was Tent-a-coose, a slave who was later ransomed by the Hudson's Bay Company, and lived at Fort Langley. He saw the blowing up of the *Tonquin*. It was his favorite story, and with delight he told how more than 200 Clayoquots perished in that blast, while others were mutilated. He saw the white men slide down the rigging, and the next morning he watched as Lewis, standing on the deck, lured the Indians to their doom.

So it was that while the causes of attack were different, the technique of the Indian warriors was similar in these two massacres. Both were possible only because proper vigilance was not observed.

Kendrick's Laundry

When the _Lady Washington_ visited the Queen Charlotte Islands in 1787 nobody expected trouble. But all had overlooked the Captain's laundry. When the gunfire stopped more than fifty Haida were dead.

The story of how the personal laundry of Captain John Kendrick of Boston led to a desperate fight off the shores of the Queen Charlotte Islands in which half a hundred Haida braves were killed, and Kendrick and his men had a miraculous escape from a similar fate, is revealed in old records in the B.C. Provincial Archives at Victoria.

It was in 1787 that a group of Boston merchants outfitted the ship _Columbia Rediviva_ — usually known simply as "the _Columbia_" — and the _Lady Washington,_ a sloop, as the first trading expedition under the flag of the United States to the North Pacific Coast of America. Captain John Kendrick was given command of the venture, sailing on the _Columbia._ Later, however, he exchanged commands with Captain Robert Gray, a competent navigator, and thereafter operated the smaller vessel. In the sloop Kendrick was able to enter waters in search of furs where it would be unwise to take the larger craft.

John Kendrick was a man of quick temper and hasty action; men either admired him greatly or detested him thoroughly. He was by turns tolerant and considerate to his men and associates and, again, a bully.

The Boston vessels carried the striped and bespangled banner of the Republic into these western waters for the first time. British traders who had come in the wake of Captain James Cook, discoverer of the potential wealth that existed in the sea otter trade, were striving with the Spaniards for control of the area. Kendrick plunged into the struggle in support of the Spanish. The result of this partisanship was to win the limited approval of the Spaniards for a time, but their favor brought him under suspicion of other traders. So it was with native chiefs, too. Some almost idolized this peculiar Yankee sea-dog, while to others he was anathema.

In the summer of 1790 he had been trading off the Queen Charlotte Islands — which the Americans called "Washington Isles." There he had done well in what is now known as Houston Stewart Channel, which he referred to as "Barrell's Sound." Koyah was the head chief of the channel that runs between Kunghit and Moresby Islands. He was a Haida chief who had been friendly with the white traders, particularly with Kendrick.

One morning as the *Lady Washington* lay at anchor in front of Koyah's village a report was made to the captain that his linen, that had just been washed, had disappeared from the line on which it had been hung to dry.

The captain was in a particularly nasty mood. He flew into an unreasoning rage. Koyah and Schulkinanse, another powerful chief, had just come on board the sloop. The infuriated Kendrick, seeing them, ordered that they be seized. As sailors held the indignant natives, Kendrick, pointing at his cannon, ordered that it be dismounted. When this was done, he had a leg of each chief clamped into a trunnion bearing, thus holding the unfortunate victims of his wrath "in stocks." He kept them there for a long time while he strode up and down in front of them, upbraiding and threatening them with worse punishment if his laundry was not immediately returned.

The missing garments were produced as soon as the chiefs could communicate with the shore. Even then his anger did not completely subside. He made them pay reparations in sea otter skins for the insult and in payment of one or two small articles which he asserted were not brought back.

Realizing that he had effectively terminated any chance of further trade with Koyah and his people, for the present at least, he held the chiefs on board until all skins in the village had been brought on board for sale. These he paid for at the tariff that had been in effect before his laundry had been stolen, for John Kendrick considered himself to be a just man. Then he left for China.

Early in June 1791 the *Lady Washington* once more nosed into the bay opposite Koyah's village. It was a suave and friendly Kendrick who greeted the Haida chief. The white man was filled with great ambitions. He planned to buy vast tracts of land in different favorable localities and thus dominate trade for the time being, and eventually attain political as well as commercial power. So it was that the captain greeted Koyah and Schulkinanse with the buoyant enthusiasm of a real estate speculator. He was delighted to find that apparently they bore him no grudge, and the matter of the captain's laundry was not mentioned. They bartered a few skins and went away.

Early next morning the two chiefs and a large number of other

Indians came out to the vessel. They brought many fine black sea otter pelts. They were permitted to board without question, and a brisk trade for knives was soon under way.

Gradually the chiefs worked their way towards the quarterdeck where the arms chests were located. Too late it was noticed that the keys had been left in the locks. Suddenly Koyah gave a triumphant shout and sprang on top of one of the chests. From beneath blankets and cedar bark mantles daggers flashed, and other weapons appeared. One giant Haida waved a marlinspike attached to a wooden handle, while squaws handed up spears and war clubs from the canoes. A brave threatened Kendrick with a war club, holding it above him, awaiting the signal from Koyah to strike.

Captain James Cook at Nootka Sound on Vancouver Island in 1778. From Nootka, Cook sailed for the Orient with sea otter pelts he had bartered from the Indians. The pelts proved very valuable, a fact which Cook noted in his journal. When the journal was published and news of the potential bonanza spread, traders sailed for Nootka and other Indian settlements, intent on capitalizing on the rich pelts which could be acquired for cheap trade goods.

But Koyah was in no immediate hurry to kill the white man. He wished to see him squirm in fear, and to taunt him before ending his life. Holding his leg up, the Haida motioned to it and called on Kendrick to put him in the stocks now. While the chief was enjoying this sport, more and more of his fighting men were swarming up the vessel's sides. Women, too, came to kill and pillage. One squaw, described as a "veritable Amazon," clambered into the main chains and from there shouted orders and encouragement.

As Koyah delayed the intended massacre to bait Kendrick, some of the seaman managed to get to the companionway and drop below decks. Koyah suddenly noticed them and sprang off the arms chest to follow. As he stepped down the companionway, Kendrick jumped on his back. Together they crashed to the bottom of the ladder, the Indian slashing at the white man with his dagger, but fortunately only piercing the captain's clothing. Kendrick dodged away and Koyah escaped to the deck.

The officers and men managed to find one or two muskets, several pistols and a couple of swords. Armed with these and led by Kendrick, they sallied forth on deck again, firing into the mob of savages. The Indians fell back and the whites managed to regain possession of the arms chests which, to their amazement, they found to be unlocked, although the Indians had taken the keys away.

While those who had arms maintained their bombardment of the Indians, other officers and men secured muskets and pistols. Then a cannon was turned around and loaded with grape shot. At point blank range it was fired into the massed savages. The carnage was terrible. Before the stunned and wounded and dying braves could recover from this death-dealing blast, Kendrick ordered his men to charge. They sprang forward with swinging cutlasses. The Haidas fled in terror, jumping overboard or dying on the deck. The last Indian to shout defiance was the woman in the main chains, who, bleeding from a dozen wounds, finally dropped into the sea. Neither she nor a number of others — male or female — reached shore, for a deadly fire was commenced upon the canoes and those seeking to swim to the beach. Then the *Lady Washington* was warped around and her big guns raked the village, blasting and splintering and demolishing the big cedar houses and reaching into the forest cover where the Indians fled for protection.

Just how many Haidas were killed in that bitter fight will never be known. According to accounts from some of those present, or who were in the vicinity, more than fifty were known to have been killed. No fatalities occurred among the whites.

The whole terrible affair was caused because of Captain Kendrick's laundry.

15

The White Slave of Slaves

In 1794 the Haida attacked the *Resolution,* murdering ten of her eleven-man crew. The survivor was forced to lie on the severed heads of his companions. Then he was made a slave to the Indians' slaves, kept naked even during the winter and not permitted to warm himself around a campfire.

Treachery, cunning and savage cruelty marked the slaughter of all but one of the officers and men of the American vessel *Resolution* off the Indian village of Skedans, Cumshewa Inlet, in 1794. The sole survivor was spared to a life of servitude, from which he was rescued by an expedition formed for that purpose.

The full story of this fiendish happening of the earliest times on the British Columbia coast has been buried in the yellowing pages of the original log book of the British brig *Ruby*. This priceless record is now carefully preserved in the B.C. Provincial Archives at Victoria. Captain Charles Bishop, of the *Ruby,* heard the details from the lips of Captain Thomas Burnett of the *Mercury,* of Providence, R.I., and from the freed slave, a sailor named Bears, when the vessels met at Nootka in 1795. He at once set the whole narrative down in the log book. The amazing story that follows is taken from that account, with necessary changes in spelling and modernization of place names sufficient to facilitate identification.

Cumshewa was head chief over the shores of the inlet that now bears his name in the Queen Charlotte group. He was a bold warrior and with his fighting men waged constant warfare on his neighbors. His main village was at Skedans, long since abandoned. His brother, Scatseye, was equally brave and bold, but even more crafty and cunning than Cumshewa. They had met the white traders on a number of occasions and coveted the riches that these strangers carried in their great winged canoes. If opportunity offered, they reasoned, it would be easy to kill these pale skinned people who were so eager to obtain the sea otter skins that were so common to the Indians, and then to take possession of the rich stores with which the vessels were laden. So Cumshewa and Scatseye were constantly on the alert to take any advantage that might be offered.

Captain Josiah Roberts arrived on the North-West Coast in command of the fine brig *Jefferson,* of Boston, some time in 1793 or 1794. He brought with him, in frame form, a tender which was assembled in the early summer of 1794 and named the *Resolution.* Command was given to one of the officers of the *Jefferson,* named Burling. He was given a complement of ten men, including Solomon Kendrick, son of Captain John Kendrick, who led the first United States trading venture to the North Pacific.

The *Resolution's* first cruise was to the Queen Charlotte Islands where the Haida Indians were known to have many fine otter skins. It was in the early summer of 1794 that Captain Burling, proud of his fine new schooner, and his men waved adieu to their friends on the *Jefferson* and disappeared into the summer haze — never to return. Captain Roberts and other traders he encountered could not obtain an inkling for months of the mystery that surrounded the *Resolution.* She had vanished completely and possibly had foundered.

Suspicion was directed towards Cumshewa nearly a year later when he tried to surprise a group of white men forming a watering party from the British ship *Phoenix,* Captain Hugh Moore. The party was attacked and one seaman killed. Captain Moore warped his vessel broadside to the beach and opened fire with his big guns. To his astonishment this bombardment was returned from the village of Skedans and with such vigor that the *Phoenix* at last drew off.

About the time of the attack on the *Phoenix,* the *Ruby* visited the Skedans, but the watchfulness of Captain Bishop afforded the treacherous Indians no opportunity of surprising the crew. Trade with Cumshewa was dull and was soon terminated. The *Ruby* then sailed northward where the mystery of the missing *Jefferson* was solved. On June 21, 1795, at Kaigani (on modern Dall Island, Alaska) Chief Kow, an inveterate enemy of Chiefs Cumshewa and Scatseye, told of what had taken place off Skedans the previous year.

"He informed me," Captain Bishop wrote, "that Cumshewa . . . had cut off a brig belonging to Boston, the captain's name, 'Paulin,' 'Pullen' or 'Burley,' and killed all the crew but one man, a sailor, which he keeps at his house."

There were a number of trading vessels in North Pacific waters at the time, and Captain Bishop passed the story along to every captain he met. Kow, too, further publicized the report, and it was not long before the treachery of Cumshewa was common knowledge.

The *Ruby* returned to Nootka, a general rendezvous for shipping, in September. The *Mercury* was riding at anchor, and

The Haida village of Skidegate in the Queen Charlotte Islands, July 1878. Although the Haida were fearless warriors who paddled their huge cedar canoes several hundred miles southward to Puget Sound to kill and pillage, their bravery — and their canoes and villages — were futile when matched with the cannon of the white men's "winged canoes."

Captain Burnett, with his supercargo, a Mr. Gardin, came on board the *Ruby* to astonish him with the tale of adventure in which the *Mercury* and *Despatch,* another Boston vessel, had gone to the rescue of the white slave of the Haidas.

"This was executed with the desired success," Captain Bishop wrote in the *Ruby's* log. He went on to tell how Scatseye, his family, and one of Cumshewa's sons were captured. In effecting this, he said, "there were several lives lost on the side of the natives; and the women fought with a degree of desperation unequalled. Having secured their prisoners, they demanded then the sailor, whose existence was denied by every one for a long time, but at last on a promise that their lives would be sacred, and seeing the humanity of their conquerors, in dressing their wounds, &c., one of the women confessed that he was chained to a tree in the woods.

"The man who owned the poor fellow as his slave was brother to the only native that was killed in the attack on the vessel, and when a division took place of their booty, he was decreed to him as a sacrifice in the name of his brother. This native demanded all the accumulated treasures of Scatseye to redress him, and which was paid the next day, when the sailor was brought on board the *Mercury* by two women in a canoe.

"It will naturally be supposed his joy on this occasion would exceed all bounds. It was not so; he was, in fact, insensible to it, so worn down by grief and cruelty, he had scarce strength to ascend the side of the ship, and sitting down on the deck, on his hams like the natives, expressed his feelings in a broken manner with a mixture of his own and the native language, and it was not for some days afterwards that he was enabled to give any account of his captivity . . . .

"It appeared that the vessel they cut off, and this man belonged to, was a schooner, consort of a Captain Roberts in a brig belonging to Boston. She was manned with 11 men and anchored at Cumshewa's some time in July '94; the Natives came off in great numbers and before the crew could put the vessel in a posture of defence, they rushed in and killed them in an instant. This man was filling powder into cartridges and before he had time to look on deck the shout of the savages announced his misfortune."

From other sources it was learned that the sailor's name was Bears. Continuing the narrative of the man's captivity, Captain Bishop went on; "He hid himself away in the hold while they were taking the dead bodies on shore, and then they fell to work rifling the vessel, and which they did effectively by the morning. Amongst the last articles that they removed in the hold, they discovered him in a cask. Instant death was what he expected, and what he said he wished. They, however, took him on deck, and then a long debate took place whether he should live or die. At length it was settled as I before related, and he was carried on shore in irons."

After giving revolting details of the manner in which the bodies were mutilated by the Indians, Bears told of how he was forced to stretch himself to rest on the dismembered heads of his companions. The next day he was compelled to carry the remains of his friends back on board the schooner. It was then set on fire and burned to the water's edge.

"To write this man's misery during his captivity would fill many sheets," Captain Bishop commented. "Suffice it is to say that in every respect he was treated as a slave of their slaves. He was stripped quite naked and kept so while with them, not even a maro (loincloth) about his waist. If he twisted one up of rushes, it was torn from about him with that savage inhumanity which distinguishes these people from the race of human kind.

"When ever a ship appeared in sight, he was dragged into the wood and chained to a tree. The winter, the only one he had the unhappiness to spend amongst them, was remarkably favorable (but most severe in cold); during this time he was forced to cut wood, make their fires, and then (was) driven from the sight of it outside the hut, and not even allowed to approach the slaves' fire but to bring them what they wanted."

From Bears the traders obtained considerable information about the habits and customs of the Indians, and Captain Bishop gives the sailor's account of the manner in which the natives conducted inter-tribal warfare. In some detail he related how he accompanied his masters on a foray against Skidegate, a powerful chief. Bears was a spectator of the battle in which Cumshewa was defeated with the loss of eleven killed and eight wounded, who were taken prisoners. Skidegate lost eight of his followers.

Four years after the liberation of the white slave of the Haida's another Boston vessel, the *Eliza*, dropped anchor off Cumshewa's village. To the Indians, however, she appeared to be a "King George ship," for she flew British colors. This deception, however, was with a purpose for the grim faced officer who scanned Skedans with such interest bore a name that was familiar to the Indians, "Captain Burling." He was a brother of the slaughtered commander of the *Resolution*. He had been at Kaigani, and there Kow had told him of the manner of his relative's death. He had also been informed that neither Cumshewa nor Scatseye would board a vessel bearing the striped United States flag. It was Scatseye that he particularly desired to capture, for it was the brother of the great Cumshewa, Kow said, who had personally killed the *Resolution's* commander.

At last Scatseye ventured on board the *Eliza*. He was instantly overpowered and the craft immediately hoisted sail and headed north. Straight to Kaigani the vessel went, and there Scatseye was turned over to his inveterate enemy, Kow. The massacre on board the *Resolution* had been partially avenged.

CHAPTER FOUR

The Captive Armourer

In March 1803 the *Boston* dropped anchor in Nootka Sound on Vancouver Island's west coast. Two days later the Nootka killed twenty-five of the twenty-seven sailors on board. Their heads were severed and lined up for one of the survivors to identify.

Maquinna, renowned chief of Nootka Sound, had been pampered and petted by the traders who had come to the North Pacific seeking furs. He had risen to great heights of influence and affluence. He had been the friend of Captain George Vancouver, and the house guest of the courtly Quadra, commandant in the days of the Spanish occupation of the Sound. When Nootka ceased to be a place of political and commercial importance, and the sea otters were less plentiful in adjacent waters, the greatness of Maquinna declined. The occasional white visitors did not pay him the attention that the aging ruler believed to be his due.

Maquinna saw in this lack of deference a cause for bitterness. He brooded over his lost magnificence. Trivial inattentions and unintended slights were magnified in his mind to purposeful insults. He searched his memory for justification for his growing hatred of the white man. He remembered that one of the earliest who had appeared in the wake of Captain Cook, Hanna of the *Sea Otter,* had turned the guns of his ship against the Nootkans when a petty theft had been committed. Then there was a captain, and Maquinna only could recall that his name sounded like "Tawnington," who had raided his village of Yuquot during his absence, in search of furs. Nor could he ever forget how Martinez, the Spaniard, had murdered the companion of his youth, Chief Callicum. These memories grew vivid; the thousands of kindly acts and fair dealings of a multitude of honest, considerate white men were forgotten.

Such was the mental attitude of Maquinna, Lord of Nootka Sound, when in March 1803 the ship *Boston*, Captain John Salter, from the great New England seaport of that name, dropped anchor in the Sound. Including the captain, Chief Mate B. Delouisa and Second Mate William Ingraham, the personnel of the *Boston* numbered twenty-seven. Amongst the crew was John Jewitt, a young English blacksmith who was carried as armourer. Another was an older man named John Thompson, the sailmaker.

Captain Salter gave warm welcome to Maquinna when the old chief came on board. He invited him to dinner, and then presented him with a double-barreled musket. The chief was so delighted he forgot, for the moment, his growing dislike of white men.

The next morning Maquinna brought the gun back. He had broken one of the locks, and he complained that the weapon was "bad." Unfortunately, Captain Salter was feeling unwell. He flew into a temper, seized the gun, and making an insulting allusion — forgetting that Maquinna understood English — threw the broken fowling piece down the hatchway to Jewitt to repair.

Maquinna clutched his throat to keep his anger down and fingered his dagger, but said nothing. Instead he went ashore to discuss with his people the treatment accorded to him. That night there was a war party. Maquinna took no part. This was a decision for his fighting men to make, for them to say whether their chief should accept this insult. As he sat huddled in his best blanket and the dancing flames cast alternate flickering light and shade over the painted faces of his people, orators urged the removal of the indignity by blood. At length battle-scarred old Yahpanetz rose and offered to make one of a war party. His father was among those who had died in front of Hanna's guns, and his spirit called loudly for revenge. One after another the chiefs and the warriors followed — all except old Topashottah, who boldly asserted that he could not forget the favors the white strangers had bestowed upon him.

The following morning Maquinna returned to the *Boston*. His purpose was dark, although his mood was gay. He skipped and danced about the deck of the vessel to the amusement of the unsuspecting white men. He was wearing a big wooden mask carved to resemble the head of a bear, and carried a whistle. "When are you intending to sail?" he asked the captain.

"Tomorrow," replied Captain Salter.

It would be a wise thing, Maquinna advised, for some of the crew to go to Friendly Cove where the salmon were running and secure a supply of the fish for food on the forthcoming cruise. The idea was a good one, Salter agreed. He ordered Mr. Delouisa to follow it out. The mate did and, taking nine men with him, started away. Friendly Cove was several miles distant.

The consequences were recorded in a diary kept by John Jewitt, one of two sailors who survived the following events:

"The steward was on shore, washing the captain's clothing; the sailmaker was in the main hatches at work upon the sails; I was in

Scenes which were familiar to
captive John Jewitt: interior
and exterior views of Nootka
dwellings at Friendly Cove on
Nootka Sound, and a Nootka
man and woman.
The drawings are by artist
John Webber who visited
Nootka Sound as one of
Captain Cook's crew in 1778.

the steerage cleaning muskets. About one hour after the boat was gone, the Captain told Mr. Ingraham to hoist in the long boat, saying there was a sufficient number of natives on board to help pull at the tackle to assist her in. When they had got the boat half way up, the natives seized every man by his tackle fall, and likewise the captain; threw him over the quarter-deck, and killed every man with his own knife, taken out of his pocket, and cut off their heads and threw the bodies overboard."

The party that had gone fishing, and the unsuspecting steward, were followed and murdered. Jewitt says that he was alarmed at the scuffle on deck and ran to see what had happened. As he climbed up the ladder from the steerage he was seized by the hair and struck on the head. He fell back unconscious. When he regained his senses, he found that he was a prisoner — and apparently the only one. He was ordered on deck to identify the heads of his companions. There was one missing — that of John Thompson, the sailmaker.

Maquinna offered life to Jewitt if he would work for him as a slave. The chief had seen the young man plying his trade and was fascinated by his skill in making daggers, spears and cutting tools. He needed just such a worker. Jewitt had no alternative; it was slavery — or death. Jewitt agreed. The first order of his new master was to direct the movement of the *Boston* from the place of attack to Friendly Cove, several miles away, where the ship could be more conveniently pillaged. Jewitt showed the Indians how to shake out the sails, then steered the vessel to the cove where she was beached.

That night Thompson was discovered hiding between decks. The Indians dragged him on shore to Maquinna, who was going to order his death, when Jewitt interposed. He asserted that Thompson was his father and boldly declared that he did not want to live if the old sailmaker was slain. Reluctantly, Maquinna agreed to spare Thompson's life, and he was condemned to share Jewitt's lot as a slave. In looting the vessel, the Indians in some way set it on fire and a major part of the cargo was lost, although the powder and some supplies had been removed to Maquinna's house.

The chief was just in dealing with his white slaves. He became really fond of Jewitt, and tolerated Thompson because of his regard for the younger man. Jewitt did everything that he could to win favor with Maquinna, knowing well that without the protection of that powerful prince his life would not be safe for a day. The lesser chiefs hated the white slaves.

Jewitt and Thompson were not the first white captives enslaved by the Lord of Nootka. There had been six sailors from a ship named the *Manchester* who had deserted and come to Maquinna for assistance in hiding from their officers. When the vessel sailed they found that they were held as slaves. One day Maquinna told Jewitt how these men had tried to escape. With the exception of a boy named "Jack," they had fled in a canoe at night. They were captured,

A portrait of Chief Maquinna painted by a Spanish artist, probably between 1785-95. Maquinna welcomed Captain Cook in 1778, and later became a friend of explorer Captain George Vancouver.

At left is a photo of a dagger Jewitt made while he was a prisoner. It is today on display at Alert Bay Museum on Cormorant Island.

The two sketches on the opposite page show the *Boston* at Nootka Sound, and Jewitt working at his forge while he was a Nootka captive.

27

brought back and executed. He showed the armourer a book bearing the names of the unfortunates. The boy was later sold to the Clayoquots, but did not long survive in the service of his new masters.

As the young armourer became acquainted with the Nootkan language he was able to hold many talks with the old chief, supplementing his knowledge of the native tongue with such English as Maquinna possessed. During one such conversation the old man told of the slights and insults he had suffered from white men. He had planned to avenge these wrongs at the first opportunity, he said, and it was unfortunate for Jewitt that such a chance came when the *Boston* appeared in the Sound and did not take sufficient precautions.

The white slaves, with difficulty, forced themselves to eat the rancid whale meat and nauseating oil with which the Indians covered their food. It was only the spectre of starvation that forced them to eat food that the natives relished. Occasionally they were able to obtain fresh fish and berries, but much of the time they — and the Indians — had barely sufficient to eat. It was during these periods of scarcity that the Indians complained against Maquinna. They looked to him to provide the community with whale meat. If no whales appeared, then he was to blame. They even plotted his death, and he appointed the white men as his bodyguards. When success was achieved in a whale hunt he was once more in high favor with his people.

Jewitt and Thompson guarded Maquinna well. They knew that the lesser chiefs feared that through them the story of the massacre of the officers and men of the *Boston* might become known, and bring reprisals upon the Nootkans. Then, too, since the destruction of the ship other trading vessels had ceased to call at Friendly Cove, the traders suspicious of what had happened to the *Boston*.

The slaves, nevertheless, did not give up hope of being rescued. They held regular prayer services in the woods, seeking Divine aid in obtaining liberty. Every time a strange Indian came to Yuquot, Jewitt endeavored to persuade him to carry word of their plight to any ship that might appear. Maquinna sensed their anxiety to escape. He sought to attach Jewitt more closely to him. He bestowed a wife upon the young man, but he, fearing that she might interfere with his plans, put her aside. On the whole Maquinna was kind to his slaves. When he had plenty to eat they were well fed, and when he had little food they went hungry.

At last one of the notes written by Jewitt and entrusted to an Indian was delivered to Captain Samuel Hill of the brig *Lydia* from Boston. Upon his return to New England in 1807, Captain Hill told of learning of the two white captives and then rescuing them. His story was published in the *Columbian Centinal,* May 20, 1807. He said, in part:

"I sailed from Newetta (Nahwitti) on the 11th of July, 1805, and arrived at Nootka Sound on the 16th. With the help of my glasses

I observed six pieces of cannon mounted on a kind of rampart in front of the village at the head of Friendly Cove. Having ascertained that there were neither men nor guns on Hog Island (which commands the entrance), I stretched into the cove and anchored in a position to command the passage to Hog Island and about two hundred yards from the village.

"In the course of twenty-four hours after my arrival I recovered the two . . . captives and the guns, anchors, a few muskets and some other articles of less consideration; these were all they had left in their possession belonging to the *Boston.*

"They were unwilling to deliver up the two men. When they were about to embark in the canoe to come on board, a council was held on the beach, wherein several of the Chiefs advised to kill them both, and hazard the worst rather than suffer the particulars of their conduct, relative to the capture of the ship, to be known; but they were given to understand that if they did not immediately bring the men on board, alive and unhurt, I would most assuredly punish their chiefs and destroy their village This had the desired effect, and I was happy in recovering the men together with the guns and ammunition, without entering into a quarrel.

"I had kept Maquinna on board until my business was finished, when I informed him he was at liberty to go."

The chief had been induced to board the *Lydia.* He could hardly avoid doing so. It was the first ship to touch there since the *Boston* was taken. His people wished to re-establish trade with the whites. The chief, however, was nervous, and asked the advice of Jewitt, who assured him that no harm would befall him. Maquinna was not sure, and asked the slave if he would give him a note to the captain certifying as to his good behavior. This Jewitt did gladly. Instead, however, of providing him with a favorable credential, the letter outlined the Nootkan's guilt and told how he and Thompson were being held in slavery. Jewitt suggested that Maquinna be held as hostage until he and his companion were liberated. Such was done.

On being returned to civilization Jewitt took up residence in New England. He published his journal. Later, he enlarged it into a book that gained great popularity. But the real tale of Jewitt's captivity — which is more akin to the "unvarnished" journal — is told around the fires of a winter night amid the Indians of Nootka Sound.

CHAPTER FIVE

Treachery at Fort St. John

As the four voyageurs stepped ashore at Fort St. John on the Peace River bullets thudded into them. The wounded men were then killed with daggers — more victims of the Beaver and Sekani Indians.

Fort St. John in 1823 stood at the angle of the North Pine and Peace Rivers. Constructed by the North West Company some eighteen years before, it had attained a position of some importance in the fur trade.

In 1820 the rival Hudson's Bay Company had opened a post in the vicinity but when, the following year the two companies united, the older establishment continued under the banner of the English concern. It was generally referred to by the traders as "St. Johns," while the Indians called it "Menahaig-O-Waskarigan," or the "Fort of the Pine," after a small stand of pine trees which grew where the rivers met.

Several forts of the same name were subsequently erected, the last one being about four miles from the modern community of Fort St. John. It was at the first establishment that a terrible massacre took place in the late autumn of 1823.

Guy Hughes, a clerk, was shot down by Indians outside the fort gate, and the following day four French-Canadians were butchered at the landing place. This massacre resulted in the abandonment of the whole district by the company for a time. All posts on the Peace with the exception of Fort Vermilion were closed.

After the union of the companies it was decided to reorganize the fur fields, many of which had become impoverished by the fierce competition that had been waged for so long between the rival trading organizations. In keeping with this planned economy it was decided to close Fort St. John and concentrate operations for a larger area at Rocky Mountain Portage (now called Hudson's Hope). Orders for these changes were given in the summer of 1823 following an inspection of the district by Chief Factor William McKintosh.

Late in October Samuel Black, senior clerk in charge at the Rocky Mountain Portage, and Guy Hughes, an assistant, arrived at Fort St. John to aid Francis Heron, master of the post, to direct the moving of merchandise and supplies to the new establishment. The Beaver Indians in the vicinity were told by Mr. Black that the place was to be closed and that, in future, they would have to carry their furs to Fort Dunvegan to exchange them for trade goods. They were not to attempt to come to the new location of the white men at the Portage. The reason for this order was that friction usually developed between the Beavers and the Sekanies when they met. The former had a contempt for the Western tribe. The Beavers made no open complaint when Mr. Black informed them of the new policy. They only asked if Fort St. John would be reopened at a later date. All partook of a farewell drink of rum with the white men and then they moved off.

Black and Heron were pleased at the manner in which the Indians received the news of the closing of the fort. Goods were piled into canoes and these started up the river in advance of the officers who had their separate craft. They did not learn until several days later that one of the cargo canoes was fired upon shortly after leaving the fort. The attempt to kill the company's servants was made by a young Sekani who had been adopted by the Beavers when a small boy. The bullet narrowly missed one of the men.

When Black and Heron departed on the night of October 28, they left Guy Hughes with two men at the fort. Hughes was not popular with the natives, but no one suspected that any of them planned his assassination. He had been instructed to arrange for some Indians to hunt to supply caches of food for the Company's canoe-men travelling the 400 miles between Rocky Mountain House, at the Portage, and Fort Dunvegan.

Hughes found that the Indians were unwilling to enlist for the service. At last one young fellow agreed to become a guide to the caches. Hughes patted him on the shoulder and commended him for accepting. The native died that night, a fact that was later blamed on the white man's touch. The other Indians complained that they were not to be permitted to hunt for the new establishment, and contemptuously declared that if the white men were foolish enough to depend upon the efforts of the Sekanies as huntsmen they would soon starve. Despite reluctance of the Indians to help, Hughes was not suspicious. On the last day of the month he sent the two voyageurs who had remained with him to Fort Dunvegan with a load of merchandise. He was now alone.

On November 1 he went down to the river to talk with a Beaver and the Sekani youth — the same one who had fired on the cargo

The top two photos show the new Fort St. John post in 1875, and a painting titled "At the Portage" by H.A. Odgen. The scene was a familiar one across Western Canada during some two centuries of the fur trade. When Antoine Rivet and his three voyageurs were murdered at Fort St. John, their canoe would have been carrying similar goods.

When the original Fort St. John was closed, an alternative fur-brigade route through the Yellowhead Pass was used with Jasper House, at left in 1872, as a rendezvous point. The area is today Jasper National Park.

canoe, a fact that Hughes did not know. Just what was discussed between the white man and the Indians remains a secret. As Hughes turned to re-enter the fort, the Sekani drew a pistol from beneath his blanket and fired. The bullet entered the back of Hughes' head and he crumpled to the ground, badly wounded. The Beaver stepped forward and shot him through the body, killing him.

Six Indians were believed to be implicated in the plot, although others may have connived in it. The natives entered the fort and started looting the small amount of property that remained. Then they attempted to set the buildings on fire. But the flames were extinguished by some other Indians who were more friendly to the Company and had already prevented the assassins from throwing Hughes' body into the river.

While these tragic events were taking place at Fort St. John, two heavily laden canoes were approaching from Rocky Mountain House. The first, and largest, was in charge of Antoine Rivet, who had grown grey in the fur trade. He had three younger men with him— Andre Morin, Pierre Montoin and Francois Toin. In the second craft were three more experienced voyageurs — Marando, Miette and Gregori. This canoe was damaged and Marando and his companions complained when they had to run ashore to repair it. In doing so they saved their lives.

Old Rivet and his crew, expecting to find rest for the night at St. John's, started to sing one of the old boat songs as they approached the end of their journey, their paddles keeping time with the happy tune. They ran the canoe in to the landing place. There was no sign of life about the fort, but it did not arouse their suspicions. They stepped ashore and drew the canoe a little way up the beach and secured it.

Suddenly a volley of bullets rained down upon the men from the branches of a tree and from behind the big fur press. The three men fell, Samuel Black reported to the Company, "and Rivet, only, spoke, and his words, I hope, will be remembered by every White Man in the country, — 'Fire, you dogs, but you will never make me afraid.' " Then, he, too crumpled and fell. The murderers now rushed forward and completed their foul work with daggers. Then they threw the bodies into the river.

The killers — the father and four sons of one family, and the Sekani youth who had shot down Hughes — now commenced to pillage the canoe that was laden "with fineries" for Fort Dunvegan. It was dark by this time and they carried on their work by the light of torches.

Meanwhile, Marando, Miette and Gregori had repaired their canoe and recommenced their descent of the river. They did not sing, being annoyed with the delay. They saw the flare of the torches and their keen eyes noted that Indians were moving about the canoe. Ominously, there was no sign of Rivet or his men. Marando held up his hand, and silently the trio slid their craft into the deeper shadows close to shore. Slowly they drifted closer. Now they could see that the savages were plundering the cargo. Quietly the three turned their canoe and started back up the river. They landed a short distance upstream where Marando sought out an Indian whom he could trust. Miette and Gregori scouted towards the fort and then climbed the steep slope to the plateau high above the river.

The friendly Indian confirmed Marando's worst fears in respect to the death of Hughes and the attempt to burn the fort. Then the native accompanied him close enough to the landing place for them to see the bullet holes in Rivet's canoe, around which the murderers were holding barbaric revel. The courageous French-Canadian and his Indian friend then crept into the fort to ascertain if property of any value remained. After this dangerous inspection, Marando, on the advice of the native, made his way up the slope to join his companions. They now started overland for Fort Dunvegan with news of the massacre.

Upon the arrival of the exhausted trio at the fort, couriers were at once sent to other posts with news of the atrocity. Indignation flamed high throughout the Athabasca fur fields, and many were the hasty plans for revenge suggested, but all had to be abandoned. It was evident that the whole Beaver tribe was not implicated, but only a small section, and therefore punitive measures must be restricted to the guilty.

It was soon learned that the killers had fled to the mountains, and to search them out of their hiding places there would require more men than were available in the whole West. Now the Indians became bolder. They sent word, through other tribes, that they intended to attack the New Caledonia brigade in the passes of the Rocky Mountains. They also intended to attack the new establishment at the Portage, they said.

In view of these threats and the killing of a man at Fort Dunvegan in the following spring by a Beaver Indian, it was decided to abandon all the posts on the Peace River, except Fort Vermilion. So Rocky Mountain Portage and Dunvegan establishments were closed. This decision required that a new route for the New Caledonia brigade had to be found. Communications with the posts west of the Rockies had formerly been carried on through Peace Pass. It was decided to use Yellowhead Pass, through which the Columbia brigades could travel as well, making Jasper's House a sort of rendezvous. So it was that Fort St. John was closed. Not until 1874 was a new establishment of that name constructed on the banks of the Peace River.

CHAPTER SIX

New Caledonia Conflict

In 1858 James Douglas became the first governor of the Crown Colony of British Columbia. But had not Chief Kwah, the powerful ruler of the Carrier Indians, shown compassion, Douglas would have been executed on a summer day in 1828.

Murder in the night at Fort George (now Prince George) in 1823 started a series of violent events that played a part in the subsequent development of the Pacific North-West. James Douglas, a central figure in the drama, was forced to leave the precincts of New Caledonia to preserve his life, and commenced a new phase of his remarkable career that led to knighthood.

Following the union of the Hudson's Bay Company and the North West Company in 1821, the fur districts of the West were re-organized. New brigade trails were laid out and speed and efficiency of transport became matters of importance. In New Caledonia — now known as Central British Columbia — plans called for the location of an active post at the junction of the Fraser and Nechako Rivers. It was to be known as Fort George and was to be commanded by James Murray Yale — "Little Yale" he was called — who was to have with him an interpreter and two men. In the summer of 1823 Yale started erecting the buildings of the establishment. He employed two Carrier Indians to help in the work.

Building operations were well advanced in August when Yale decided to pay a quick visit to Fort St. James, on Stuart Lake, the headquarters of New Caledonia, to obtain additional tools and supplies required to complete his fort. He took Joseph, the interpreter, with him, leaving Du Plante and the other French-Canadian and the two Carrier Indians, Tzill-na-o-lay and Un-la-yhin, to continue construction.

In the absence of the clerk, the two Indians took liberties that they would not have attempted if Yale had been present. Du Plante undertook to reprimand them and they did not like it. He said that he would inform the fort commandant of what had happened during his absence. That night, while Du Plante and his companion were asleep, the savages stabbed them to death. Then they cut off their heads, picked up a few articles and fled.

The main band of Indians in the neighborhood, the Takulies, a branch of the Carriers, were not implicated. They would not move the bodies, for fear that they might be suspected, nor did they touch a thing in the store or dwelling.

Un-la-yhin made his way to the east of the mountains where two years later he was killed by Cree Indians. Tzill-na-o-lay disappeared and no trace of him could be found, although the HBC made diligent search for him. Five years passed without any word of the fugitive. Then in the summer of 1828 Chief Kwah, the powerful ruler of the Carriers who lived on Stuart Lake, was host to a great gathering of Indians. They came from all parts of the Carrier country, and were entertained in a lavish manner by Kwah and the people in their main village a mile or so from Fort St. James. Since William Connolly, chief factor in charge of New Caledonia, was absent, James Douglas, the young clerk who had recently married Connolly's beautiful daughter, was left in charge.

Late on the night of July 31 when the Indian village was quiet — Kwah had taken his guests on a grand hunt, leaving only a few old men, women, and children — an Indian woman stole from the sleeping camp and made her way to the fort. She whispered to the guard at the gate that she wished to speak to Mr. Douglas. The man laughed and told her that he was asleep. But she was insistent. She said that she had some important information that she would not impart to any other person.

At last the guard had Douglas awakened. He came out to the woman. "Well, what is it?" he asked.

The woman motioned him farther away from the guard. Then standing on tip-toe beside the giant Douglas, she whispered: "Tzill-na-o-lay, who killed the men at Fort George. . . ."

Douglas was alert in an instant. "Yes!"

"He is here," she went on. "He is hiding in the village. You come and get him." Then she disappeared into the darkness.

Later in the morning the Indian village was just beginning to stir when Douglas appeared with several men and started to search the lodges for the wanted man. No one was found, although every house in the village was inspected. It looked as if the elusive Tzill-na-o-lay had again evaded capture. There was only one suspicious circumstance in the search — a woman in one lodge had continued to pack bundles when the place was inspected. Douglas decided to return there.

"Search this place thoroughly," he ordered, then moved closer to inspect a dark corner. As he did so, an arrow was thrust forward

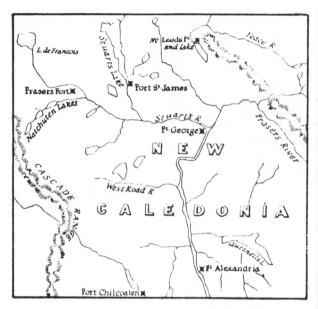

New Caledonia in 1858. At right are James Douglas and the grave of Chief Kwah who spared Douglas' life. When Kwah died he left four wives and sixteen children.

Below: A pack train leaving Fort St. James and Kwah's great war dagger that was used to threaten Douglas.

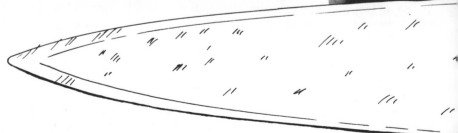

ᑐᐅᑕᐤ ᐁᐧ
ᐁᐸᐸᐱ

1755 ᐱ ᐊᐸᐧ ᐁᐧᐱᐅ
1840 ᐊᑐ ᐱ ᐨ ᐁᐅ

ᐃᐧᐸᑕᐤ ᐨ ᑎᐨ ᐊᐧᐳ
ᑕᐃᐧᐳᐧ ᐅᐧᐧ ᐅ ᐰ ᑌ
ᐨᐧᐁ ᑐᐃᐧ ᑐᑎᐧ ᐸᐧ
ᐅᐧ ᐰᐰ ᑕᑐᑐ ᐧ ᐳ
ᑐᑕᑐᐧᑐ.

HERE LIE THE REMAINS
OF
GREAT CHIEF
KWAH

BORN ABOUT 1755
DIED SPRING OF 1840

He once had in his hands the life of
(future Sir) James Douglas, but was great
enough to refrain from taking it.

from the shadows. Douglas dodged, then plunged forward and seized the murderous Tzill-na-o-lay. A desperate struggle followed, only ending when one of the men struck the Indian on the head with a musket and felled him.

In his old age, Sir James Douglas made reference to the capture of the Indian in a letter to his daughter, in comment on a newspaper story of it: "True, I seized the Indian . . . and secured him after a desperate struggle, but I did not shoot him with my own hands, he was afterwards executed for his crimes." But at the time, Douglas reported to Connolly that "the accomplishment of a much desired event" made it necessary for him to write. This event was "the death of Tzill-na-o-lay whom we dispatched on the first of this Month, in the Indian village of this place, without confusion or any accident happening to any other individual."

In any event quick justice was meted out to the murderer. But in "dispatching" Tzill-na-o-lay in the Indian village Douglas made a grave error. He was sufficiently conversant with Indian customs to have known that by doing so he was involving Kwah with his guests. Violation of sanctuary placed responsibility upon the host.

When Kwah returned he was indignant — not because the murderer had been executed, for he agreed that he was deserving of death — but because the penalty had been exacted within the bounds of his village. He brooded over it for several days, then in a swift and sudden move he and his warriors invaded the fort. The personnel of the establishment had no chance. They were captured, the men being huddled into the main trade hall. Despite his desperate efforts, Douglas was bound hand and foot, and his life threatened with Kwah's great war dagger held above him by an Indian who awaited word to plunge it into the white man — but Kwah did not wish to kill Douglas. He demanded goods to recompense the relatives of Tzill-na-o-lay. Douglas refused. Kwah replied that he had plenty of time. He and his warriors waited. Eventually he obtained what he wanted, and Douglas was liberated.

Chief Kwah was satisfied. He had obtained the means for restoring his prestige. The friends of the dead man, however, were not ready to accept the goods as wiping out the debt of blood that they held against the white clerk.

Early in December they acted. Several months before Governor George Simpson had made a ceremonial visit to Fort St. James and chided Kwah for his part in capturing the fort. But Douglas had asked the governor to forgive his friend, Kwah, and all had ended happily. There had been no demonstration, and it was thought that the affair was closed. So Douglas, with several men, started for Fraser Lake where John McDonnell was in charge.

Nothing happened until they were within sight of the fort. They stopped for a moment at the village of Natleh, about two miles from the pickets of Fort Fraser. Then they crossed the little river that drains the lake into the Nechako just as 120 Indians, mostly from Noolah, a populous village near modern Vanderhoof, suddenly

Fort George, above, and Fort Fraser photographed in 1876 by George M. Dawson of the Geological Survey of Canada. They had changed little in the years following the attack on James Douglas in 1823 and disappeared in the early 1900s. On the site of Fort George, however, rose Prince George, the largest city in Interior B.C.

appeared. They were in a threatening mood, and it was not long before Douglas found their threats were directed against himself.

It would have been easy for him to have hastened to the fort, but to do so would have brought the mob in pursuit to the stockades. In such an event a clash would have been inevitable. Douglas stopped. He spoke quietly to the three men with him. They, too, halted and primed their firearms. Then they calmly waited until the armed and painted warriors crossed to the little plain where they stood.

What happened when, instead of running, this tall white man stayed to face 120 Indians is recorded in the journal of Fort St. James for December 9, 1828:

". . . Mr. Douglas relates a most atrocious attempt which was made against his life in passing through the village of Natleh on

Fort St. James in 1911. It was destined to survive longer than any other of the Hudson's Bay Company posts in Western Canada. Today a National Historic Park, it is being restored to the period of the mid-1890s. Buildings which have been restored or reconstructed include the Fish Cache, Men's House, the massive General Warehouse, Trading Shop and Office. In addition, a modern interpretive centre provides background on the historic outpost.

the 3d inst., when he was surrounded by about 120 Indians, a great number of whom announced their intention of killing him and appeared fully prepared to perpetrate their infamous design, in which, however, they were prevented from succeeding, partly through the interference of the Fraser's Lake Indians with Yazecho and some other well disposed people, but mostly by his own good and prudent conduct and the determination he evinced of selling his life dear should no other expedient be left of determining the affray.

"Mr. Douglas with his three men faced them with presented arms and allowed them to exhaust their rage in threats, and did not quit the field until the rascals had all dispersed. This conduct was the most prudent he could have followed, for if he had retreated towards the Post (about two miles distant from the spot where this scene was exhibited) he would no doubt, have been followed thither by all the villians by whom he was assaulted, and the affair would not have terminated without bloodshed ... And the cool and determined courage which Mr. Douglas evinced on the occasion must have impressed the vile rogues with a higher opinion of the Whites than they ever before entertained of them. As they were all disguised, the principal actors in this scene could not be discovered, but it is being ascertained that the Indians of Natleh did not interfere, further than endeavoring to prevent bloodshed. The blame of the whole must rest upon those of Noolah, and Thluch leh of Fort George."

The situation did not improve. The Indians of such places as Noolah and Thluch lehs — which was a village on the Nechako, near Fort George, — were determined to kill Douglas. He had to be constantly on his guard. On February 27, 1829, Chief Factor Connolly wrote to Governor George Simpson about it:

"Douglas' life is most exposed among these Carriers," he said, "He would readily face a hundred of them, but he does not much like the idea of being assassinated. With your permission, he might next year be removed to the Columbia; where ever he may be placed he can not fail of being essentially useful."

With this testimonial, James Douglas went to the Columbia department headquarters at Fort Vancouver, where he proved so "essentially useful" that he became the chief assistant of Dr. John McLoughlin, and succeeded him as the head of the Hudson's Bay Company's Board of Management west of the Mountains. Later he moved to Fort Victoria, where he became governor of Vancouver's Island and later of British Columbia. His wisdom and courage made possible the solid foundations of those colonies — and all because of that murder in the night at Fort George in 1823. It is possible that if the Indians had not sought to avenge the execution of Tzill-na-o-lay upon him, Douglas would not have gone to the Columbia when he did. In that event he might never have risen above the command of a fur trading district.

CHAPTER SEVEN

Attack at Fort McLoughlin

The HBC post of Fort McLoughlin was well protected with a stockade and corner bastions but, incredibly, water had to be carried from outside the walls. This weakness did not go unnoticed by the Indians.

Fort McLoughlin was a strong, although isolated, Hudson's Bay Company trading post on Campbell Island, Milbanke Sound. It was erected in 1833, the third of three establishments formed on what is now the British Columbian coast, to meet the competition of "Boston traders" — as the maritime fur buyers from United States were known. Fort Langley was the first, constructed in 1827; Fort Nass — later renamed Fort Simpson — was next in 1831; and two years later Fort McLoughlin was commenced. Into its construction went the experience gained in building the other posts.

It was roughly 140 yards by 150 yards in size, its palisades strongly built of eight-inch logs, mortised into squared logs at both top and bottom, and surmounted with stakes. Its houses were substantial. It had two bastions and galleries. But there was an incredible weakness about this fort — no good drinking water was available within the enclosure. Water had to be carried from outside the walls. This fact led to a surprise attack upon six men who formed a watering-party not long after the fort was completed.

Donald Manson was the officer in charge. He was an experienced trader, aged about thirty-five. He had as his chief assistant and second in command a well educated and resourceful youth of nineteen, Alexander Caulfield Anderson. Another young officer was John Dunn, who ten years later wrote a history of Oregon that is recognized as a valuable source book. Anderson was replaced by another brilliant young man, Dr. William F. Tolmie. Manson had the reputation of being a strict disciplinarian, and thrashed a French-Canadian workman named Richard. The man deserted and was thought to have gone into hiding at some nearby Indian camp.

Such action could not be permitted — deserters could not be allowed to find sanctuary among the savages. The Indians, when questioned, gave contradictory answers. Manson determined to exact definite information. He seized Tyest, one of the leading chiefs of the district, and held him hostage for the return of the missing man. Trade with the Indians was stopped. They were told that their chief would be liberated when they delivered Richard at the fort, or produced authentic information concerning him.

Describing subsequent events, Anderson wrote in his history of the North West Coast: "It was a Sunday and not a soul was to be seen outside the fort, save a solitary Indian seated by a small fire on the opposite side of the bay. Evening came on, and the men asked permission to go outside for water. Reluctant to give permission at that late hour, I declined to give the keys without the sanction of my superior, which being given, the men went out, leaving two only within the fort, who were appointed to guard the hostage (Chief Tyest), and one who guarded the wicket. I myself went out, having my pistols on me, and leaving my other arms where they were easily accessible, for I had misgivings and they were very shortly realized.

"I advanced to the edge of the bank, when suddenly, within a few yards of me, I saw, darting thro' the bushes, a host of armed Indians. I turned at once, gave the alarm, and retreating to the fort was speedily prepared to defend the entrance. After having seized my arms, and on my way back to the gate, I perceived our hostage highly excited, and evidently bent on endeavoring to make his escape. As I ran I called to the guards to tie him, which they did.

"The Indians were checked," Anderson modestly stated. "One by one our men made their way toward the gate, and thro' the narrow wicket. And as they came in repaired to the bastion and commenced to fire. Mr. Mason, having meanwhile appeared on the gallery and directed their actions. Thus repelled, our assailants retreated speedily, and the gates were closed.

"On mustering our men, we found that one only had been wounded, by a severe axe blow on the shoulder, but one was missing and we supposed him dead.

"Of course, watch was kept during the whole night, all hands remaining on watch; and about nine o'clock, from amid the dense darkness, we heard a voice — the voice of our missing man — he called out to Mr. Manson; in return we asked, 'Who are you?' He responded with his name and said he was a prisoner with the Indians, tied to a canoe, and unless they were assured that their chief, our hostage, was safe, his life would be sacrificed. We summoned the chief to the bastion and made him speak to his children, deferring the interview to the following morning. The result of the whole was that, at that time, our man was restored to us, we

A.C. Anderson, above, was second in command when Fort McLoughlin was attacked, although he was only nineteen.
W.F. Tolmie, right above, relieved Anderson. Tolmie's diary with its description of the attack is in the Provincial Archives at Victoria.

The bastion at Fort Victoria, photographed in the late 1850s. An excellent description of a bastion was given by Lieutenant R.C. Mayne in his book, *Four Years in British Columbia, 1862:*
"In two of the corners (of the fort) is usually reared a wooden bastion, sufficiently high to enable the garrison to see a considerable distance over the country. In the gallery of the bastion five or six small guns are mounted, covered in, and used with regular ports like a ship; while the ground-floor serves for the magazine. . . ."

surrendering the chief in exchange, but exacting two hostages of inferior standing — slaves probably. Our man was produced clad by the Indians in an entirely new suit of broadcloth and we clothed our hostage with a blanket and some other articles of clothing."

Such is the factual account given of the attack on Fort McLoughlin by A.C. Anderson. His friend, Dr. Tolmie, who came to relieve him in December of the same year, in his diary which is in the B.C. Provincial Archives, gives additional information that emphasizes the important part that young Anderson played in repelling the design of the Indians to capture the fort. He was a remarkably good shot, and at least one Indian fell before his aim.

"Anderson was outside when the armed savages were seen rushing out of the woods in all directions," the doctor wrote. "He sped into his room and arming himself with a rifle and a double-barrelled gun, placed himself at the gate and fired three shots. Mr. Manson was on the gallery, looking out, when the men sallied forth for water and was the first to perceive the enemy and give the alarm. He then flew to the bastion, and while the scuffle was going on, fired several charges of buckshot. No other shots were fired from the fort, but showers of buckshot rattled on the East bastion from the Indians. The men, six in number, were surprised . . . They all got back safely except two, one of whom was carried off and the other broke loose after receiving a dreadful gash on the shoulder from a blow of an axe aimed at his head. As soon as the firing commenced from the fort, the Indians scampered, but several were wounded who afterwards had their wounds dressed by Mr. Manson."

While the Indians won the release of their chief and handed over two substitutes, the real problem of what had happened to Richard, the deserter, was no nearer solution. It was years later that the fate of the unfortunate man was learned.

It was reported to HBC officials by Indians that when Richard left the fort he attempted to reach an Indian village some distance from Fort McLoughlin. He was not sure of its location, and asked some native boys whom he encountered to guide him. They undertook to do so, upon condition that he give them some of his clothing. To this he agreed. After proceeding a short distance, the boys asked for other garments and then insisted that he divest himself of still more clothing. This he refused to do, and in order to force him to comply, the boys started throwing stones at him. They eventually stoned him to death.

Fort McLoughlin was later abandoned when Fort Victoria was established. In 1849, when it was decided to start coal mining near the north end of Vancouver's Island, Fort Rupert was constructed. The majority of the Indians who had formerly clustered about the post on Milbanke Sound moved to the vicinity of the new establishment. Today nothing remains of Fort McLoughlin.

CHAPTER EIGHT

Finlayson's Strategy

In 1844 Tzouhalem the Bold, a fierce warrior chief of the Cowichans, sallied from his lair to pillage and kill. Unfortunately for his plans, he met another bold man, Robert Finlayson, the twenty-six-year-old clerk in charge of Fort Victoria.

Tzouhalem, the fierce warrior chief of Cowichan, decided to visit Ku-sing-ay-las, the place where the strong willow fibers were obtained. He wanted to see what the white men had done since they started to build a fort there the previous year. They called it Fort Victoria.

Although he came in peace he was prepared for war. He knew how much tribesmen whom he had terrorized hated him. But it was curiosity, not plunder, that impelled Tzouhalem to visit Chief Tsil-al-thach of the Songhees, who had moved his village from its age-old location on a beautiful bay (now Cadboro Bay) facing the strong currents that flowed about the southern tip of Vancouver's Island. The new home of Tsil-al-thach, he had been told, was not far from the new fort. He wished to ascertain why the Songhees had abandoned their fine fortified lodges and ancestral totems to reside at a place of the white man's choice where fishing was poor and where there were few clam beaches.

The Cowichan had seen white men before; he did not like them. He had visited Fort Langley on the Fraser River, where he had tried unsuccessfully to shoot the commander. He could not fathom these arrogant strangers who dressed in garments that were not made from animal skins, cedar bark, nor woven from dogs' wool.

It was in the late summer of 1844 that Tzouhalem obtained his first sight of the log stockades as he entered the harbor of Camosun. Beyond it rose the smoke from the Indian lodges. He liked the

Songhees' new village. It was to the north of the fort, on a gully through which a small stream trickled from the swamps where willows grew abundantly.

Tsil-al-thach was absent when Tzouhalem arrived, but that did not worry the Cowichan. He simply assumed command of the place, and none dared disobey his orders. He walked through the thick bushes between the village and fort to obtain a closer view of the white man's post. He was interested in forts and had a strong one of his own at the entrance to Cowichan Bay. After studying the stockades and the octagonal building that projected from the angle he was not particularly impressed. But he was surprised to see strange animals grazing in an open space close to the fort. They were not deer, although some had two horns. They appeared tame for some were dragging a queer vehicle, while a white man walked beside them shouting and occasionally beating them. These big animals, larger even than an elk, should make good meat Tzouhalem concluded. He ordered several to be killed.

Roderick Finlayson, "the young, fair-haired chief" as the Songhees called him, had heard of Tzouhalem the Bold, who sallied from his lair to kill and pillage. Finlayson had only recently assumed command of Fort Victoria following the death of his superior, John Ross. But despite his youth, Finlayson soon proved as courageous as the fierce Tzouhalem.

When he was informed that several horses and oxen had been killed, Finlayson lost no time. The gates of the fort were closed, and every preparation made to meet possible trouble. Then he sent a message to the village, demanding the surrender of those who had slaughtered the cattle, and payment of the value of the beasts.

Tzouhalem laughed at the interpreter who relayed the message and returned an insulting reply. The land belonged to the Indians, he argued, and the animals that fed upon it were also theirs. Now let Finlayson take up the story as he related it in a private autobiography:

"I then suspended trade or any dealing with them until this matter was settled; whereupon they sent word to some of the neighboring tribes to come to their assistance, as they intended to attack the fort. In the meantime, I kept all hands at their arms, set watches night and day, to prevent surprise."

The Songhees were a strong tribe. Their village and those of their allies were scattered along the shoreline from beyond Sooke to Mill Bay and on the San Juan islands. Canoes filled with warriors came with every tide. After several days during which time Tsil-al-thach, who had returned, pretended to negotiate, an imposing horde had gathered.

Then, Finlayson said, "they fired upon the fort, riddling the stockades and the roofs of the houses with their musket balls. It was with the greatest difficulty that I could prevail upon our men not to return the fire but wait my orders.

"After a close firing of about half an hour, I spoke to the

The interior of Fort Victoria in the late 1850s. In 1844 the buildings were riddled with musket balls when the Songhees Indians defied youthful Roderick Finlayson, inset, who was in charge but who refused to become involved in a revengeful retaliation.

principal chief, informing him that I was fully prepared to carry on the battle, but did not like to kill any of them without explaining to them that they were wrong and giving them another chance of making restitution.

"A parley ensued among them, during which I sent our Indian interpreter out to speak to them, telling him to make it appear that he had escaped without orders and to point out to them the lodge that I was determined to fire on, and for the inmates to clear out. This they did at the suggestion of the interpreter who, upon making a sign to me, as agreed upon, that the lodge was clear, came towards the stockades and was admitted into the fort by a back gate.

"Seeing that there was no sign of them coming to terms, I pointed one of our nine-pounder carronades, loaded with grape shot, at the lodge, which was a large one built of cedar boards . . . fired! The effect was that it was completely demolished, the splinters of the cedar boards flying in fragments in the air. After this there was an immense howling among them . . . but my plan, I was happy to find, had the desired effect. I was aware that those Indians had never seen the effect of grape shot fire from a cannon."

"After the excitement was over," went on Finlayson, "a deputation of the chiefs called and were asked what they wanted. They desired to parley with the white chief. I then arranged with them that if two or three of them came within the stockades to make arrangements with me, I would send out two of our men as hostages, to which they agreed.

"I then fully explained to them that I had it in my power to destroy all their houses and kill many of them, and I did not like to do so; and it was fortunate for them that none of our men were shot; that I was determined to have the offenders punished or payment made for the animals they killed. They preferred the latter, and before that day closed furs to the full amount were delivered at the gate, after which, on smoking the pipe of peace, with promises on their part that the animals would not, in the future, be molested. So we parted good friends; trade was resumed as formerly."

There was great discussion and argument around the fires in the big houses that night. Tzouhalem was not convinced of the white man's power. The whole thing might have been a trick, he said. He wanted to see if the young white chief could repeat the demonstration of destruction with the great thunder-making gun.

"The chiefs, next day," Finlayson related, "wanted to see more of the effects of the big gun in an amicable way.

"I told them to place an old canoe in the harbor, and that they would clearly see the effects. So they did. I then loaded one of the guns with a cannon ball and pointed it at the canoe in the harbor, and fired. The ball passing through it, bounded over the harbor and afterwards into the woods beyond. This news spread far and wide and had a very salutary effect on them."

Now Tzouhalem was satisfied. He shrugged his shoulders, called his men together and paddled away, leaving to Tsil-al-thach the remorse of failure and the loss of face that went with it.

Not long after this occurrence the Indians accidentally set fire to the bush near their village. The wind carried the flames towards the fort. The alarm was sounded and under Finlayson's directions the whites fought the menace and finally extinguished the fire. The carelessness of the natives annoyed the young white chief. His neighbors were too troublesome and as long as they were located on the same side of the harbor as the whites they were a potential danger. So Finlayson suggested to Tsil-al-thach that he move his people across the water.

The Indian potentate was indignant, but the white man was adamant. Tsil-al-thach did not have the daring Tzouhalem at his elbow now — and there were those terrible cannons. He at last agreed, provided that the whites helped him to move. The fine village at the foot of Victoria's present Johnson Street of which Tsil-al-thach was so proud was torn down and rebuilt on the opposite side of the harbor, directly across from the fort.

CHAPTER NINE

Fort Rupert Murders

In 1850 three Nahwitti braves approached some white men to warn them that the fierce Haida were reported to be coming on a raid. This gesture of friendship resulted in murder and an attack on the Nahwitti by British warships.

Government by the Crown in the Colony of Vancouver's Island was ushered in by a strike, murders and Indian conflict which required the assistance of units of the British navy to restore order. The focus of this unrest was Fort Rupert, established by the Hudson's Bay Company in 1849 to give protection to collieries opened near the north end of Vancouver's Island. Coal miners were brought from Great Britain to work in the mines.

In March 1850, Governor Richard Blanshard arrived at Fort Victoria to read the proclamation inaugurating the Colonial government. His was to be an unhappy life during the year and a half that he remained in the colony. He received no salary and no allowance for expenses, even though cost of living was high. Another frustrating problem was that the majority of the white inhabitants of the island were employed by the HBC and looked to its officials for instructions. The result was that the unfortunate governor had little to do, except spend his time in hating the HBC, which he blamed for all his woes.

Not long after his arrival he received complaints from the Fort Rupert miners. They were not satisfied with the wild game and fish provided for their meals; they also demanded beer, spirits and new wine as part of their daily rations. When such changes were not made, they refused to work.

Governor Blanshard appointed Dr. J.S. Helmcken, the young doctor at Fort Rupert, a magistrate. But Helmcken could obtain no co-operation from the discontented miners, who were anxious to end their contract with the Company. This desire was heightened by the news of the discovery of gold in California. The lure of the new Eldorado drew men from all parts of the Hudson's Bay fur fields. When the bark *England* reached Fort Victoria and discharged cargo, she was ordered to proceed to Fort Rupert for a cargo of coal for California. Three members of the crew of the HBC's ship *Norman Morison* deserted and hid on board the sailing vessel, hoping to reach the gold regions.

When the vessel arrived at Fort Rupert the miners soon learned that there were deserters secreted on board. They, too, desired to take this opportunity of joining the stampede to California. After some planning with crew members they also deserted and joined the vessel on her departure.

Loading the cargo of coal, in the absence of proper wharves and other facilities, was slow. Some days after the *England* dropped anchor off the fort, the steamer *Beaver* hove in sight. Believing that the paddlewheeler had come in search of them, the deserters left their hiding place and took refuge in the woods. The *Beaver,* however, did not stay long. When she had gone Dr. Helmcken told Captain Brown to get word to the sailors to return to the ship as it was unsafe to remain in the forest where they were isolated and might be attacked by savages. This friendly warning the men believed to be for the purpose of trapping them. Tragically, they ignored the advice.

The Indians of the region were the Nahwitti branch of the Kwakiutl nation which formed a bulwark against attack from the fierce Haidas and Tsimpshean raiders to the north. The Nahwittis were courageous and hot tempered. Part of the band had settled near the fort, but the main body maintained its traditional hold at the northern end of Vancouver's Island.

Three Nahwitti braves and a boy were paddling in the vicinity of Shushartie when they saw three white men on the shore. It had been reported that Haidas from the Queen Charlotte Islands were coming on a raid along the coast. The Indians were friendly towards the whites. They paddled towards the strangers to tell them to be on their guard against the murderous pirates from the North.

The sailors did not appreciate the kindly purpose of the Indians. One of the deserters raised an axe and waved it threateningly, while another picked up a stone and threw it at the approaching canoe. This hostility incensed the Nahwittis. They landed and pursued the now badly frightened men into the forest, where they were easily overtaken. The savages cut them down. Two of the deserters — brothers Charles and George Wishart — were stabbed to death, their bodies hidden in a hollow tree stump and covered with brush. The third sailor, Fred Watkins, was stabbed and his body weighted and sunk in the sea.

When word of these killings reached Fort Rupert, the miners became more agitated. They refused to take part in the defence in

Fort Rupert, shown above in the late 1860s, was established in 1849 when coal was discovered on Vancouver Island near present-day Port Hardy. Afterwards Kwakiutl Indians settled around the Fort, below, resulting in several confrontations with the whites.

At left is Dr. J.S. Helmcken, who was appointed a magistrate and faced several hundred muskets when he demanded the surrender of the three braves accused of murder.

the event of a general Indian uprising and demanded that the post be abandoned without delay. They, themselves, moved in a body to Shushartie. Now local Indians took advantage of the helplessness of the officials and the few loyal men remaining. The natives climbed the palisades to leer down at the unhappy whites, who realized that any demonstration would be the signal for an attack. Just when the situation appeared to be desperate and the Indians were becoming bolder, the providential arrival of the Company's vessel, *Mary Dare,* with reinforcements, changed matters. The miners were persuaded to return to the fort.

The *Mary Dare* was followed a few days later by HMS *Daedalus,* Captain G.R. Wellesley, carrying Governor Richard Blanshard who had come to display the authority of the Crown. On October 11, the day after the arrival of the warship, Magistrate Helmcken, with a fearless French-Canadian interpreter named Battineau, volunteered to go to the main village of the Nahwittis. They were to demand the three braves accused of the murders. It was a dangerous undertaking.

As Helmcken's canoe approached the village several hundred muskets were pointed at him. He did not hesitate, but landed and addressed Chief Nancy. The old chief, after conferring with other head-men, admitted the guilt of the tribal members, but offered to settle the matter in Indian fashion by reparations. This offer the magistrate rejected.

On his return to Fort Rupert, Magistrate Helmcken reported to Governor Blanshard and Captain Wellesley. The civil power, as represented by Helmcken having failed, Captain Wellesley decided to take action — naval style. He sent Lieutenant Burton with armed boats to enforce the surrender of the fugitives. The boat expedition landed several miles from the village as night was falling — and, incredibly, lit fires. Next morning at daybreak they took to the boats and dashed in to capture the village, only to find that every Indian had fled in the night. The astonished lieutenant, in accordance with his instructions, set fire to the village and destroyed all the canoes he could find. He then returned to the warship.

The *Daedalus* could remain at Fort Rupert no longer since she was running short of provisions. Governor Blanshard was left to make his way back to Victoria as best he could, and the warship started for San Francisco. As she ran towards Cape Scott a Bella Bella canoe was sighted. One of the Indians fired a shot. The *Daedalus* stopped, lowered a boat and fired a cannon in the direction of the natives. The Bella Bellas did not understand that the shot was an order for them to halt. All they could comprehend was that a boat was rapidly approaching. They opened fire and wounded an officer and two sailors. This episode ended the pursuit because food stocks in the warship were so low that she could not remain in the area.

Not until July 1851 did the navy again appear at Fort Rupert. This time it was HMS *Daphnae,* Captain Fanshawe, that came to enforce the Queen's law. Lieutenant Edward Lacy was given charge of an expedition against a new and strongly fortified camp that the Nahwittis had built on a small island in Bull Harbour. James Douglas, the chief factor of the HBC, in a letter of August 6, 1851, described the affair:

"The Newettee (Nahwitti) affair has not yet been fully disposed of although they have been rather severely handled by a boat party of 60 men and officers from the *Daphnae,* who surprised their village and carried it by assault, in the midst of a severe fire from the Natives — with very trifling loss, say two men slightly wounded, who have since recovered.

"The native position was very strong, and protected with stockades, which they thought impregnable, and were consequently rather surprised when they saw it carried by a body of white faces. They, however, contrived to make their escape, by some secret passage, with the exception of 5 or 6 killed and wounded, the chief Nancy being, unfortunately, among the former.

"All their property and provisions were captured and destroyed together with about 20 fine canoes — so that they have sustained a very severe loss. The tribe is now completely dispersed and are reported to be some where on the West side of the Island."

Governor Blanshard, who had accompanied the *Daphnae,* now offered a reward of thirty blankets for the capture of the wanted men. The Indians had turned against their fellows, blaming them for the punishment that had fallen upon the entire tribe. They tried to get them to surrender and, when they would not, killed two of them. The third man made his escape, so they killed a slave to complete the number, and delivered the bodies at the fort gate. They claimed the reward which the officer in charge of the fort was not authorized to pay. He did give them a letter to the Governor, certifying the receipt of the bodies.

Whether the Indians were ever paid is not known; nor is it known whether the unhappy Blanshard paid the account of £47 15s. (some $250) which the Admiralty rendered for his passage on HMS *Daedalus* to Fort Rupert in 1850. Blanshard had had enough of trying to govern such a wild and inhospitable land for nothing. On his return to Fort Victoria, he resigned and left on board the *Daphnae* when she sailed to the south.

To this day in the homes of the Nahwittis, when the fires burn brightly and the waves break on the bar, the old story tellers recall the two attacks made upon the tribe by the navy.

The Basis of Freedom

The first jury trial in what is today Western Canada was held on the pioneer steamship _Beaver_ in 1853. The capture of the culprits, however, nearly resulted in war with the Cowichans.

Trial by jury — the right of every British subject since the day that the barons of England forced King John to sign the Magna Carta in 1215 — came to the North Pacific Coast in 1853 when two Indians were charged with murder. The court was held on board the pioneer steamer _Beaver_ at Nanaimo, and the result was the conviction and execution of the accused.

It was an important event, for on that raw January day the old system of justice administered by rule of thumb — no matter how impartially it had been measured — ceased. It was fitting, perhaps, that the prerogative of free men to have their guilt or innocence determined by their peers or equals should have been extended first to two uncivilized subjects of the Crown. No better example of the meaning of "democracy" in a new country could have been desired.

The Hudson's Bay Company maintained a sheep station at Lake Hill, Saanich, some four miles from Fort Victoria. The great fur-trading organization was vitally interested in the humble arts of agriculture and animal husbandry, and in colonization, for they had been given a grant of Vancouver's Island. Among the men they employed in the age-old occupation of shepherds at the Lake Hill station — or as it was also called, "Christmas Hill" — were Peter Brown and James Skea. Good, reliable young Orkneymen they were.

On the morning of November 5, 1852, it was the turn of Skea to drive the sheep out to pasture, and for Brown to remain at the station to do the many chores at the hut that served them as home. Just as Skea was leaving several Indians made their appearance. This arrival caused no alarm, as visits from natives were frequent.

Skea returned about noon, expecting to sit down to a meal of his friend's cooking. But as he approached the house he noticed that there was no smoke rising from the stone chimney. Brown might have taken ill, he reasoned as he hurried along the path that led to the dwelling. When he could obtain a full view of it he stopped, then hastened forward. The lifeless body of his fellow shepherd was sprawled on the ground outside the door. He had been shot several times in the chest.

Since his companion was beyond human aid Skea hurried to Fort Victoria for assistance. He was soon on his way back with a number of armed men. A careful search was made of the vicinity, but the killers had vanished. They had, however, left several valuable clues — a fire bag, looking glass, comb and Indian pipe, dropped while they looted the cabin during their flight.

It was necessary to the safety of the Colony that the murderers be apprehended, Governor James Douglas declared. He at once instituted an intensive search for information that would lead to the identity of the assassins. Finally word was brought to him that one of those responsible for Peter Brown's death was a Cowichan, while the other was the son of a Nanaimo chief living at one of the villages on the river of that name.

Fortunately, about then HMS *Thetis* under Captain A.L. Kuper arrived from the British naval base at Valparaiso. Having by now learned the identity of the Indians who had killed Brown, Douglas opened negotiations with the chiefs of the tribes to which they belonged, demanding their surrender. He kept Captain Kuper advised of what he was doing. Writing to the captain under date of December 21, he said that some chiefs were willing to comply with his order, but that the friends and relations of the accused were definitely opposed to handing them over to the white men. "I am now convinced," declared the governor, "that the surrender will never take place unless they are intimidated by the presence of an overwhelming force." Douglas planned a demonstration and raised a small force of French-Canadian halfbreeds from the employees of the HBC. He also arranged for the Company's steamer *Beaver* and the brigantine *Recovery* to be made available as transports for the service of the Colony. Having completed these preparations, he requisitioned a force from the *Thetis* in support of civil authority.

Captain Kuper immediately responded with 130 sailors and marines under command of Lieutenant Arthur Sansum, with Lieutenant John Moresby as his second in command. Governor Douglas, as commander-in-chief of the Colony, took personal charge of the expedition.

In a subsequent report to London Douglas wrote:

"The expedition anchored off the mouth of the Cowegin

The *Beaver*, pioneer steam vessel on the Pacific Coast, at Victoria in 1862, and Nanaimo in the early 1870s. Here on the *Beaver* in 1853 two Indians were found guilty of murder and hanged the same day at the harbour entrance. The bastion shown in the photo was built in 1853 as protection for coal miners from attack by Indians and still stands today.

(Cowichan) River on the 6th of January (1853). I immediately des-
patched messengers with an invitation to the several Native Tribes,
who inhabit the valley and banks of the river, to meet me as soon
as convenient, at some fixed point, for settling the differences that
had led me to visit their country; at the same time giving them
distinctly to understand that I should be under the painful necessity
of assuming an hostile attitude, and marching against them with
the forces under my command should they decline my invitation."

The chiefs replied that they would meet Douglas the following
morning near the river mouth. Consequently, shortly after daybreak,
the sailors and marines were landed. It was a miserable day, with
a cold drizzling rain softening the snow that had covered the
landscape. What was considered to be a favorable position, in the
event of trouble, was selected and occupied.

Several hours later the dull thud of war drums in the distance
heralded the coming of the Indians. Then, around a bend, they shot
in their great cedar war canoes, their faces painted, and all armed.
They sprang ashore, the deer hoof fringes of their leathern battle
dress clicking. "And last of all," said Douglas, "arrived two large
canoes, crowded with the friends and relatives of the murderer,
hideously painted, and evidently prepared to defend the wretched
man, who was himself among the number, to the last extremity.

"On landing they made a furious rush towards the spot where
I stood, a little in advance of the force, and their deportment was
altogether so hostile that the marines were, with difficulty,
restrained by their officers from opening a fire upon them. When
the first excitement had a little abated, the felon, fully armed, was
brought into my presence, and I succeeded after a great deal of
trouble, in taking him quietly into custody; and sent him, a close
prisoner, on board the steam vessel."

Such was the unvarnished tale told by a central figure in this
strange drama. Another participant in the affair, Admiral John
Moresby, then the junior officer with the expedition, in his masterly
book, *The Admirals,* gives further details. He tells how the Governor,
a non-smoker, calmly lighted a pipe and seated himself on a camp
stool when the savage warriors were most threatening, simulating
such indifference to their demonstration as to confound them.

"The indifference covered some anxiety," said Admiral
Moresby, "for without an instant's hesitation a large body of braves
rushed up the hillside, taking higher ground and completely
outflanking us, a knowledge of tactics rendered somewhat
disquieting by the array of glittering eyes and gun barrels covering
us. I desired to move our men, but it would have been ticklish work
just then, and permission was refused."

At last Douglas' pretended indifference and lack of fear had
its effect. The chiefs intimated that they would parley. In describing
the conference, Admiral Moresby said:

"Not a sound by the Governor's voice. Then a chief lifted his
spear, advancing a step, all the warriors brandishing their weapons

The Cowichan Valley Indian village of Quamichan, and Cowichan canoes. In their big, seaworthy craft the Cowichans for years murdered both whites and Indians among the Gulf Islands.

and rattling their loin-ropes, till the noise was as the crackling of a forest fire. At the first word dead silence fell, and the Governor calmly resumed his pipe, an attentive hearer."

After two hours of argument during which Douglas endeavored to inculcate the principles of democratic justice and personal responsibility, the fugitive was surrendered. In reporting to the Colonial office, he pointed out that his aim was to impress upon the minds of the chiefs "that the terrors of the law should be let loose on the perpetrator of the murder only, and on no other members of the Tribe, except such as should be found resisting the Queen's authority and protecting them from Justice, but that was a matter so different from their own customs in such cases and so foreign to their ideas of propriety, that it was exceedingly difficult to make them comprehend our views."

Having secured the arrest of the Cowichan brave, the expedition went on to Nanaimo. In answer to a peremptory demand for delivery of the wanted man, the chiefs tried to temporize. They offered reparation for the killing of Brown. Some of the older men were willing to give him up, but his friends and relatives refused. They did not welcome democracy.

After several days of tedious negotiations, Douglas explained: "I therefore decided upon adopting more active measures and with that view, ordered the immediate advancement towards the Nanaimo river, where the villages are situated. We accordingly pushed rapidly in that direction, but the boats had scarcely entered the river before their progress was arrested by the shallowness of the stream, about ¾ of a mile before the first village. The troops were, never-the-less immediately landed, and the movement was so rapid, that before the Indians had recovered from their consternation, we succeeded in carrying the stockade, without firing a shot."

Here again Douglas' leadership was successful. Lieutenant Sansum wished to attack the strong fort, but Douglas realized that to do so would inevitably result in the loss of lives for well armed and determined warriors were manning the galleries that ran around the inside of the 20-foot-high palisades. The wall was built of logs, and provided with loop-holes for musketry, after the manner of the white man's defensive works. After surveying this formidable looking fortification, Douglas ordered the naval officers to attempt to have the launch and pinnace, still shoaled at the river mouth, brought up. These boats carried small brass cannons.

Lieutenant Moresby was entrusted with the task. After great efforts by the sailors the boats were pushed and shoved across the bar into the channel. They arrived, several hours later, and turned their guns towards the fort. In the meantime both white and red men had stolidly watched each other. The natives knew that the "big guns" of the white men were deadly. They had been told of what had happened when the lodges of the Songhees were blasted by the carronades of Fort Victoria; and of the devastation of the Nahwittis' villages by those of the navy only two years before. When the sailors, under Lieutenant Sansum's instructions, started to load the guns, the sliding gate of the stronghold slowly rose.

The Governor with several officers and men immediately entered. The place had capitulated; a weird scene greeted them. Fires burned slowly on the earthen floor of an immense lodge, casting dancing shadows on the drab walls and over the impassive faces of the savage warriors.

Douglas decided to spend the night there. It must have been a fantastic sight, as white sailors and painted braves, neither of whom could speak the language of the other, danced about the fires in mutual entertainment during the sleepless hours. The next morning another village, higher up the river, was taken. Here it was learned that the wanted man was in hiding near a small stream a mile or more to the west.

Basil Battineau, the fearless French-Canadian interpreter, and eight of his half-breed scouts and sixteen sailors were detailed to hunt him. J.W. MacKay, the Hudson's Bay Company officer in charge of the new establishment of Nanaimo, in telling of the eventual capture of the Indian, said:

"A few inches of snow had fallen, and his footprints being traced to where he had descended to Chase River to allay his thirst at the stream, his trail was followed to where a heap of driftwood crossed the bed of the little river. Here the scout Basil Battineau, who was on the Indian's track, found himself at fault, and as it was after sunset and getting dark, would have abandoned the search had not the Indian, who was hiding under the driftwood, snapped his revolver at him. The cap and gunpowder in the charge were damp and neither exploded. The scout followed the direction of the sound, but in the gloaming could not distinguish the object of his search. In the meantime the latter tried a second shot, when the cap only exploded, the flash thereof indicated his hiding place. The Indian was discovered, knocked down and handcuffed in an instant."

The final act of tragedy, as described by Douglas himself: "The two Indians now being in custody, they were brought to trial, and found guilty of wilful murder, by a Jury composed of the officers present. They were sentenced to be hanged by the neck until dead, and the execution took place in the presence of the whole Nanaimo tribe, the same appearing to make a deep impression on their minds and will, I trust, have the effect of restraining others from the commission of crimes . . . ."

Such, then, are the facts as obtained from fading records in the B.C. Archives, of the manner in which the first jury trial came to be held in what is now British Columbia. The place at the entrance to Nanaimo's beautiful harbor where the two Indians paid for their crime in the white man's manner is known to this day as "Gallows Point."

CHAPTER ELEVEN

Hell's Gate Aflame

Among the rocks and trees above the rapids of the Fraser Canyon war erupted in 1858. Upwards of 200 Indians and miners died, the headless bodies of the miners tossed into the river.

Conflict between white miners and Indians had been a constant dread in the mind of James Douglas, Governor of Vancouver's Island and Chief Factor of the Hudson's Bay Company, since it became evident that some 800 ounces of gold he had sent to the San Francisco mint on the Company steamship *Otter* in February 1858 had started a stampede. The first miners arrived in early spring and by early summer some 30,000 had turned the former Hudson's Bay Company fur preserve into a name known around the world. By summer trouble had materialized and savage warfare flamed through the rock-bound canyons of the Fraser River. Headless bodies floated down above Hell's Gate. White miners stumbled into Fort Yale to tell of having been shot at by Indians. Men quit the river bars and retreated to the trading posts of Fort Yale and Fort Hope. Wild excitement gripped all, and it was impossible to differentiate between truth and falsity, for factual accounts struggled with lurid rumor for mastery.

Just how many men died in the short, sharp, cruel war fought amid the rocks and trees that lined the turbulent Fraser gorge above Hell's Gate will never be known. For miners' estimates ranged up to 100, and the same for the Indians. There were several causes contributing to the uprising. In the first place, the natives resented the white strangers who invaded their country and dug into its soil. They complained, too, that their families had not been respected and their homes had been violated. Undoubtedly, the sale of liquor to the natives was regarded as a direct source of trouble.

The miners early recognized the danger of supplying intoxicants to the Indians. They held a meeting at Fort Yale and made regulations aimed at preventing the natives from obtaining alcoholic beverages. They were stringent rules. One provision adopted was that unlicensed purveyors of liquor should be seized, stripped and given thirty-nine lashes on the bare back. They were then to be driven from the place. Unfortunately, these measures came too late. The Indians were preparing for the warpath. They were becoming bold and insolent, even on the lower part of the river.

On July 26, a report reached Fort Langley of the killing of several white men and the capture of a white woman by natives near the mouth of the Fraser River. A relief force was raised and sent from the trading post. Although no evidence could be obtained to substantiate the story at that time, information obtained years later seemed to confirm it. On the same day a party of 160 men, with 400 horses, on their way to the new diggings, was ambushed just south of the border in the Okanagan Valley. Three men were killed and six wounded.

Writing from Fort Yale on July 27, the correspondent of the *Victoria Gazette* asserted: "Dr. Spearm says the Indians at New York Bar were all drunk, and had driven the few whites on the Bar into one tent, where the latter were determined to make a stand, and if worse came to the worst, for all to die fighting like men. The Indians were armed with guns and knives. There were two dead bodies found in the river, presumed to have been murdered by the red devils, yesterday."

As the month of August opened, the seriousness of the situation increased. Fort Yale was crowded with men who had been forced to desert their claims between that place and The Forks (Lytton). More headless bodies tumbled through Hell's Gate and drifted through the foaming corridor. Men's tempers flared. There were those who shouted for a war of extermination, while other more temperate persons advanced the idea of trying to get the Indians to enter into peace pacts. In support they cited the manner in which the HBC obtained the confidence of the natives through fair dealing. Proponents of both the "war to the knife" and the "pacification" systems prepared to raise separate forces.

Some forty men formed themselves into a rifle company under the leadership of Charles Rouse, said to have been a former Texas Ranger. This was the first military organization recruited. The unit went up the river above Fort Yale for some miles and fought a battle with the Indians. Henry M. Snyder, the regular correspondent of the *San Francisco Bulletin,* who also contributed news items to the *Victoria Gazette,* described Rouse's campaign against the savages. Written from Fort Yale, August 17, Snyder's story appeared in the *Gazette* a week later.

About August 7, he said, two Frenchman were killed on the trail above the Big Canyon. Two days later a well armed party of forty miners left Fort Yale with the intention of forcing their way through

Ned Stout, one of five survivors of his group of twenty-five miners. Since the Indians used arrows tipped with rattlesnake poison, even a slight wound meant death. Stout was wounded seven times, and survived because the Indians had by then used all of their poisoned arrows. The photo was taken in 1913 when Stout was eighty-eight.

Opposite: Hell's Gate with salmon drying on the racks. Here Dick Green and his six companions were murdered. During the fighting the Indians left behind poisoned salmon, hoping that the starving miners would eat them.

At upper right is Fort Yale at the lower end of the Fraser Canyon in 1858. In June the bodies of twenty-nine miners were taken from the river at the Fort and another thirty-two downstream at Fort Hope. Many bodies were never recovered.

to The Forks. They were well supplied with provisions and made their way as far as Boston Bar without having a fight. A large number of white men congregated there, but they begged the newcomers to stay and help them in case of attack. They agreed to do so.

The Battle of Boston Bar was probably the first clash between whites and reds on the river where a considerable force was employed on each side. Speaking of it, Snyder said: ". . . On the 14th a fight with the Indians took place, which lasted three hours, and resulted in the complete rout of the savages. Seven of the Indians are known to have been killed, and a number wounded. One white man only was wounded, and that slightly in the arm. About 150 white men were in the fight."

Snyder also told of another fight. James Stewart, on arriving at Fort Yale, reported that he and a party of miners had been attacked at the head of the Big Canyon. He said that nine Indians, including a chief had been slain, a number were wounded and captured. The miners had found Mexican sashes on the bodies of the dead Indians. These, Stewart declared, had been taken from Cornish, Scottish and American miners. The incensed whites fired five Indian villages, burning their stocks of food.

The miners determined to put an end to the trouble. Word to the effect that a strong column was to be sent against the savages brought men hurrying to Fort Yale. Four companies were organized. Snyder, the news correspondent, had command of fifty-one composing the "Pike Guards." Later he was reinforced by thirty-one late arrivals. The "French Company," under John Centras, numbered eighty-two. There were two smaller companies, numbering about twenty men each, under leadership of a man named Graham and another called Galloway. Captain Graham's outfit was known as the "Whatcom Guards." These smaller organized bands were opposed to the policy of Snyder and Centras, which aimed at conciliation. They favored extermination of the Indians.

The Pike Guards and French Company led the way, offering peace to the natives. It was readily accepted. Graham, who followed, however, made it apparent that he did not respect the white flags that Snyder had given to the Indians who expressed a willingness to submit to the white men's authority. That night Graham's camp was attacked by Indians who killed Graham and his chief lieutenant, James Shaw.

Snyder's mission of conciliation and peace, and Graham's unhappy fate, virtually ended the organized fighting. Some idea of the desperate character of the brief conflict may be glimpsed from a narrative account by Ned Stout, given by him to the B.C. Provincial Archives prior to his death in 1924.

He was one of a party of twenty-five miners at work at Nicomen Creek which flows into the Thompson River, Stout said. They were warned by a squaw of the approaching Indian war. Having no time to lose the men gathered their belongings. They then retreated down the river and made their way in safety to a point a little below The

Forks, where the Indians sighted them for the first time.

The miners had been proceeding with utmost caution, avoiding open spaces where possible, but when they realized that their movements were being watched, they hurried ahead as quickly as possible. On Jackass Mountain the trail crossed a slide — an open area where the miners had to make a run on loose rock. Here it was that the Indians attacked, shooting down from the boulder-covered heights above the slide. Three men, including their leader, McLennan, were seriously wounded by arrows. Stout says that they were poisoned arrows, and tells how these unfortunate men died in agony the following day.

After running the gauntlet at Jackass Mountain the miners left the Indian trail and descended to the river. While progress was slower here, big boulders offered greater security. Carefully they picked their way from rock to rock and from tree to tree, taking full advantage of all natural protection. They travelled at night, when possible, and hid by day.

At Tilton Creek they found the Indians massed on the opposite bank. They attacked before dark, but were driven back. Then when darkness fell, Stout and his companions set fire to the forest, which gave such illumination as to prevent a surprise rush. They then made their way across the creek and proceeded down the river. It was daylight when they reached a position from which an unobstructed view could be obtained for some distance down stream. "Old Texas" who had succeeded to the leadership, scanned the banks with a glass. There were Indian villages in the neighborhood.

"Drop boys and hide," whispered the old frontiersman. "If they have seen us they will try and surround us; if they have not seen us, we must attack them tonight or they will butcher us tomorrow."

Fate favored them for once — the Indians had not discovered them. They hid until just about sunset, then Old Texas whispered; "Now boys look to the priming of your guns." They started their cautious approach towards a large Indian village, creeping to within 50 feet of its outskirts before causing an alarm. The Indians jumped to their feet, seized their bows and muskets and fired, without obtaining full view of the white men, who were partially hidden by the shades of the bush. The miners were at no such disadvantage for the Indians were outlined against the fires of the village. The toll of dead and wounded in that first blast from the desperate miners' guns was heavy. The muzzled loading weapons having been fired, the miners made a rush armed with short lengths of wood to which they had attached their bowie knives to form improvised spears. The Indians braves met them with their daggers. A terrible scene followed, bearded prospector and dusky native thrusting and stabbing and slashing in a turmoil of death, with savage war-whoops and Anglo-Saxon oaths increasing the din that was punctuated by occasional revolver shots. Such a struggle could not last long — a matter of minutes. Then the Indians, who had been so taken by surprise, broke and fled.

China Bluff in the Fraser Canyon
where Ned Stout and his four
companions were rescued — all
near death from their wounds.

The victors counted twenty-two dead Indians, and mourned six of their companions. The surviving miners noted that a number of dead Indians were wearing the red silk Mexican sashes favored by miners, particularly a group of Cornishmen who worked in the Little Canyon. Such sashes were not confined to men from Cornwall, however. This clothing suggested to the fugitives from Nicomen for the first time that theirs was not the first party ambushed. The remains of their friends they put in the river to prevent mutilation. Then they set fire to the village, destroying it with all its stocks of food, consisting mostly of salmon.

Gradually, day by day, the survivors continued their tortuous way, creeping and crawling from cover to cover. Each one of the fast dwindling little band was more or less seriously wounded, fatigued to the point of exhaustion and leaden-eyed from lack of sleep. Food, too, was scarce, with only a bit of dried salmon from the Indian village they had captured and some roots. At one place they saw three salmon hanging on a stick on the bank of a creek. One of the men, with a glad cry, reached for one.

"Don't touch them," shouted Mike Malahan, "they're poisoned." He pointed to several small birds that lay dead on the ground beneath the fish.

Each day saw the group diminish; each night the survivors weaker. Finally, on the flat at China Bar some twenty miles above Fort Yale, they started to build a protecting work. Here they must remain until the end; they could go no farther. Two men died that day, shot down as they worked.

The next morning the five wounded and despairing men lay behind the piled stones and brush waiting for the next assault. It would probably be the last, for they had hardly a pinch of powder left. Suddenly gun fire reverberated up the canyons from below — not far below. The embattled men looked at each other, but said nothing. Each thought he might be mistaken. Again the "ping" of a rifle, clear and sharp. "The boys are coming!" Old Texas stammered. "The boys are coming!"

Shortly after Graham's men could be seen struggling up one side of the river, and Snyder's column on the other. As they approached the emaciated, ragged, wounded and starving men rose from their "fort" to wave thankfully. Of McLennan's company of twenty-five men, twenty had died, including the leader. The five survivors were more dead than alive, with Ned Stout hit by seven arrows. He survived the ordeal and again ventured upstream. In the Cariboo Mountains he was a member of a party that discovered Williams Creek which yielded $1,000 a foot and triggered another massive gold rush. Afterwards Stout settled in Yale where he died in 1924 at 99, proud that he had never smoke or drank. He is buried in Yale's pioneer cemetery and commemorated by Stout's Gulch, just upstream from today's Barkerville.

CHAPTER TWELVE

Massacre at Ganges

In July 1860 in Ganges Harbour on Saltspring Island eight unsuspecting Bella Bella Indians were slaughtered by Cowichan warriors. Was the cause distrust of the white traders or revenge for the early killing of two Cowichans by Fort Rupert Indians?

Few who visited the peaceful places of Saltspring Island today can visualize that in earlier times settlers faced danger and death to establish themselves on its shores. The Island was first known as Chouan. Later it was officially named Admiral Island, but the custom of calling it after the saline springs at its northern end overcame all attempts to have it designated otherwise.

It was always an attractive place and it appealed to men who had been drawn to the country by discovery of gold on the Fraser River. Settlement started at Ganges Harbour and near Fernwood Point on the northeast side. These places were continually menaced by the savage armadas from the north, while the settlers had to be constantly on guard against the treachery of the rovers from the big Indian villages in the Cowichan Valley.

There were four of these villages, from which long canoes went out to search the seaways amongst the Gulf Islands and take what advantage they could of travellers. The warriors from Quamichan were especially notorious. Many a lone white man vanished, and even small parties disappeared. The secret of their fate was known only to members of that tribe or to other Cowichan braves. But they, too, had to be alert for when the mighty Haidas from the Queen Charlotte Islands, or the haughty Kwakiutls from the labyrinth of waterways north of Comox, came in their great dug-outs, they were in danger of being butchered. These fleets of savage Northmen skirted along the eastern shores of Saltspring by way of Trincomali Channel. They brought terror to the settlers, who dared not show resentment of their thieving. The white residents never knew the day nor the hour when vicious warfare would flame about them. Indian vengeance did not require that retaliation be made upon the individuals responsible for hostile acts, but only the spilling of strangers' blood.

For instance in early July 1860 some white settlers were fishing the north end of the Island. Near them were two Cowichans similarly engaged. Suddenly a fleet of Fort Rupert canoes rounded a point. The Cowichans promptly abandoned their lines and paddled to the white men's boat into which they climbed for sanctuary. The Northerners did not hesitate. They, too, came up to the boat, clambered aboard and killed the Cowichans, cutting off their heads. They did not molest the whites.

A few days later there was an even more barbaric slaughter. It involved Bella Bella Indians employed by a trader named George Macaulay, a man of experience in dealing with the Indians. But he was disliked by the Cowichans who did not trust him, claiming that he had failed to pay a debt due to one of their chiefs. It may have been this dislike and distrust that was responsible for the terrible massacre, or possibly it was in retaliation for the killing of the two Cowichans. Whatever the reason, on the morning of July 4 Macaulay was on his way to Fort Victoria from Bella Bella. He had business to transact with some of the Saltspring Island settlers and attempted to land at the northeast settlement where the cluster of buildings had gained the local name of Beggsville. But the Cowichans there made such a hostile demonstration against his crew that he abandoned the attempt and continued to Ganges.

What happened is best told in a statement Macaulay wrote a few days later:

". . . About 2 p.m. I landed from a canoe in which there were nine men, three women, and one boy, all of the Bella Bella tribe. . . . On touching the shore I fancied there was a hostile spirit envinced by a large party of Cowichan Indians on the beach. . . . I spoke to the Cowichans, telling them that the Bella Bellas were good Indians . . . and that I trusted that the Cowichans would treat them as friends. . . . They, in answer, assured me that they had no intention of molesting the Bella Bellas."

Accepting the word of the treacherous Cowichans, whom he had reason to suspect for they kept their blankets about them as if concealing weapons, Macaulay took a chance and left his crew to the mercy of their ancient enemies. For this decision he was later blamed by Governor James Douglas. He went off to call on Thomas Lineker, a settler who lived a short distance from the beach at the head of the harbor. He had scarcely reached the place when he heard outbursts of musketry. Along the waterfront he could see the Cowichans firing at the Bella Bellas as they tumbled into their canoe, and pushed off.

"It was evident to me," Macaulay went on, "that the Bella Bellas would be defeated, as the Cowichans numbered between fifty and

Settlers on Vancouver Island and the Gulf Islands were vulnerable to attack since many of their farms fronted sandy beaches, providing ideal access for canoes.

Ganges Harbour where the Bella Bella Indians were slain by the Cowichans.

sixty and opposed to them were only nine of the Bella Bellas.

"In about half an hour, three of the Bella Bellas having fallen, the canoe commenced retreating, upon which the Cowichans immediately manned their canoes and gave chase, a dropping fire meanwhile being kept up.

"The Bella Bellas threw overboard all the skins they had with them, in hopes that, to pick them up, their pursuers would lose ground, but the manoeuvre had not the desired effect, as there were a number of small canoes with boys in them, who were directed to secure the skins, whilst the Cowichans continued the chase, gaining on the Bella Bellas at every stroke of their paddles.

"As a last resort the latter made for the shore, intending to take to the bush, where they could avail themselves of the shelter afforded by trees &c., from the fire of their treacherous assailants. They succeeded in landing, and were received by another party of Cowichans who had lain in ambush at that place, expecting a movement of this kind on the part of the Bella Bellas. Being now entirely surrounded they were soon all killed with the exception of one man, who escaped into the wood, and two women and the boy, who were taken prisoners by the Cowichans."

Late that night, the wounded Bella Bella made his way to the home of Lineker, where the settler and Macaulay were keeping under cover. Lineker had sent his family across the Island. The night was being made hideous by the shouting, shooting and war-whoopings of the celebrating Cowichans. Quickly the wounds of the sole survivor of the canoe crew were bound. He had been shot through the cheek and in one arm. Then Lineker led him to the trail and instructed him how to reach the other end of the Island. What happened to him is not known.

Several days later, when the Cowichans had left the place, settlers gathered at the home of Lineker and requested him to notify the authorities. He wrote a letter to Governor Douglas. He told of the murder of the two Cowichans and of the massacre of the Bella Bellas, and asked for protection for the settlement.

Governor Douglas lost no time. He communicated with Admiral R.L. Baynes, who gave orders to Captain James C. Prevost, of HMS *Satellite*, to investigate the affair. In his report to the admiral, Captain Prevost gave an interesting glimpse of conditions on the Island:

"The settlement on Admiral Island is divided into two distinct communities by a lake three miles in length; that on the N.E. side off which I first anchored, amounts to 25 souls. The other, at the head of Ganges Harbour numbers 26, extending over between five and six miles of wooded land. Some few houses have been built and a few acres of garden ground brought under cultivation. A trail connects one end of the settlement with the other by crossing the lake in a canoe. Each settler claims 200 acres, and as many of the lots have a quarter of a mile sea frontage forming one side of Trincomalee Channel, which the Northern Indians pass through on their way to and from Victoria you will at once perceive the defenceless state of these men. Their isolated position without any acknowledged head, no one to keep order, no one to organize them, had caused a feeling of anxiety among them."

There was not much that Prevost could do. Except for the things belonging to Macaulay in the canoe, no harm had been done to any white settler, and the authorities were in no position to punish natives for inter-tribal wars. The *Satellite*, however, steamed over to Cowichan Bay, and Captain Prevost went up the river to Quamichan. He assembled the chiefs and told them that such acts of barbarity must cease. The Indians astonished him when they agreed not to make war on other tribes if the Government would guarantee that others would not attack them. The Cowichans readily surrendered a woman prisoner and restored Macaulay's property as far as they could for some of it had been sent to the Fraser River. Captain Prevost sent Lieutenant Roche across the Gulf in the warship's launch in an endeavor to gather more of the stolen property. Beyond that there was nothing to be done.

CHAPTER THIRTEEN

The Salt Whiskey War

The unprincipled traders mixed their illegal whiskey with sea water then bartered it to the proud Haida. The result was a confrontation that didn't end until the incensed Indians were shelled by a warship.

It was a bright, lazy morning in May 1861. Vagrant whiffs of wind scarcely ruffled the water and the sails of the little schooner *Laurel* flapped idly as she drifted with the current in Satellite Channel off the end of Saanich Peninsula. The captain and crew of the *Laurel* were not unduly disturbed when they saw, coming towards them around the headland, a great armada of long cedar canoes.

It was apparent from the high prows of the great dugouts that the approaching fleet was that of the Skidegate branch of the Haida tribe from Queen Charlotte Islands. These fierce warriors from the north made periodic visits as far south as Puget Sound and, of recent years, had developed a habit of spending some time on each such excursion at Fort Victoria. This visit was anything but welcomed by the authorities. The Haida were bold men and fierce fighters. Less powerful bands of Indians were frightened of them. Even the white men were not comfortable when hundreds of their unwanted guests were camped on the edge of the town. There was always the danger of a collision, if not with the whites then with the local tribesmen.

The Haidas had been particularly annoying during their stay at Victoria that spring of 1861. While there had been no concerted defiance of the law, individual cases of pilfering had been many. Now, however, they were on their way home with canoes well filled with the proceeds of their stay.

The men on the *Laurel* were no more particular how they made profits than were the savage vikings from Queen Charlotte Islands.

A keg of whiskey was hidden away on the schooner for just such a marketing opportunity. But of what use would one keg be to such a host? The *Laurel's* captain, through his glass, estimated there were several hundred Indians in the cedar flotilla. He had an idea. There was an empty keg on board. Without a moment's hesitation the container with its whisky was uncovered and half of its contents transferred to the empty keg. Then both were filled with sea water.

Chief Jefferson and several other head-men of the Haidas boarded the schooner. Did the captain have any whisky for sale? He did. He had two kegs of fire-water. A bargain was soon made. The Haidas resumed their voyage. Then it was decided that a halt should be made to test and taste the quality of the liquor.

The Indians turned. They raced back towards the schooner. The white men, frightened now, sought to row to aid their craft, for the fitful breezes did not drive them far towards land. There was no escaping the wrathful Haidas who quickly surrounded and boarded the schooner. They did not inflict personal injury to the white men, wily old Jefferson keeping his braves in hand to that extent. But the chiefs and nobles went to work in a systematic manner, stripping the *Laurel* of everything moveable. Then they angrily paddled off.

The Haidas were still mad when they rounded Saltspring Island and started up Trincomali Channel. The homes and storehouses of the pioneer settlement of Beggsville came in sight. It was probably a desire to replace the salted liquor with some that was more palatable that caused them to land. They looted the storehouses. Then, still without ardent spirits, they headed for Nanaimo. Here they stayed for a day or two and sold some of their loot.

In the meantime the *Laurel,* empty of everything but an enraged crew, managed to reach Victoria. Bitter complaint was made to the authorities against the action of the Indians — although nothing was said of the transaction that preceded the looting of the schooner.

Governor Douglas was indignant. Something drastic must be done; these Haidas must be taught to respect white man's laws. He communicated with the naval authorities at Esquimalt. Rear-Admiral Sir Thomas Maitland concurred with Governor Douglas. The natives must be taught a lesson. Lieutenant-Commander Charles R. Robson, captain of HMS *Forward,* was ordered to proceed in pursuit of the Indians.

Just as the *Forward* was about to sail, a fast canoe sped into the harbor bringing news of the happenings at Beggsville. The courier told of how Edward Mallandaine's storehouse had been raided and some property taken. Then that of Begg — the original settler — had been broken into and most of its contents taken. With this additional intelligence Captain Robson made all speed on the track of the Indians.

Now, let the story be continued by Captain Robson, as he related it to the Admiral:

". . . I was informed by Mr. Begg of the depredations committed by a large party of Northern Indians, who stopped at the N.E. settlement on the 9th instant and in broad daylight broke into a store-house of his, carrying off flour, potatoes, turnips and a flag. While thus engaged in plundering, Mr. Sampson, one of the settlers, hearing the noise ran down to the beach, but was warned off by the marauders threatening his life if he approached. Previous to this, they had broken into and quitted the house of Mr. Mallandaine, another settler. The settlers I found much alarmed."

After obtaining first hand information from the Saltspring Island community, Captain Robson followed in the wake of the war canoes. When he reached Nanaimo, the captain was given further lurid details of the wicked actions of the Haidas — some true, others magnified. Here he found some of the nautical instruments and furnishings of the *Laurel* that had been bartered to residents of Nanaimo. This action, he was convinced, established piracy upon the part of the Indians. He consulted Magistrate William H. Franklyn, who, as a former master mariner, had acquaintance with the law and lore of the sea. Magistrate Franklyn was sure that the plundering of the *Laurel* could be defined as nothing else. He called upon the captain to aid the civil power in apprehending the pirates.

Up to this time Captain Robson's instructions had been to investigate the reports made of Haida depredations. Now, however, having been formally called upon to assist the authorities it was a more serious matter. As the *Forward* hurriedly took on coal, accom-

HMS *Forward,* the gunboat which took part in the pursuit of the Haida and, as related in the next chapter, apprehending the Indians who murdered Frederick Marks and his daughter.

modation was arranged for the Magistrate and Adam Horne, an experienced Hudson's Bay Company officer who was enlisted as interpreter. Edwin Gough, a fearless coal miner, agreed to act as special constable, a position he filled in the little coal mining camp. Messrs. Begg and Sampson, from Saltspring were also on board to identify the Indians, if they could.

The gunboat made all possible speed in pursuit of the raiders, who had several days start. At last the Haidas were sighted. They had encamped by a creek just north of Willow Point on the shore of Vancouver's Island, several miles south of Campbell River, and about two miles from Cape Mudge. They had selected a strong position and thrown up temporary fortifications of logs and stones, for they were in hostile country and might be attacked by the Kwakiutls. It was 6 p.m., May 17, when the *Forward* came abreast of the place. It had been learned at Nanaimo that the Haidas numbered some 300 persons.

Continuing his narrative, Captain Robson said:

"I sent Constable Gough and Mr. Horne, both well known to them, and unarmed, on shore, with a message to say that the Magistrate of Nanaimo was on board, to enquire into the nature of certain robberies . . . and to desire the chief to come off. Failing to do so, they were to be informed, that they would be fired upon.

"The first part of the message they positively refused to obey, the second they treated with the utmost derision, saying they had

A Haida brave from Massett and, at left above, C.R. Robson, captain of the *Forward* during both encounters with the Indians. Beside Robson is the Honorable Horace Douglas-Lascelles who succeeded him as captain.

their guns and could fight and were not afraid of a 'schooner like that.' They became greatly excited, flourishing their weapons, (and) seized hold of Mr. Horne, who was afraid at one time they intended to detain him as prisoner. I then steamed close in, hailed through Mr. Horne, and warned them of the consequences of their refusal, which they only received by shouts and yells of defiance."

At last the two men on shore managed to get away from the Indians and back to the *Forward*. It was a narrow escape for them. The Haida warriors were ready to fight. They had never refused combat and they would not do so now. They held the white man's "canoe" in contempt. They numbered as many fighting men as did the warship.

"Finding all other means of no avail," the captain went on, "I fired a shot high over the encampment, which was instantly replied to by a volley of musketry direct at the ship, the balls whistling thro' the rigging close over our heads and striking the side. Of course, after this, I immediately opened fire, directing the guns to be laid for the canoes, which it was my object to destroy in preference to an indiscriminate slaughter, which might easily have been effected . . ."

The shot and shell from the heavy guns shattered trees, splintered the heavy logs that the Haidas imagined would provide them protection, and made kindling of their fine big war canoes. Such havoc had never been witnessed by the natives. When Shasha, a chief, crumpled and fell with a gaping wound in his abdomen, another leader was killed outright and others had been wounded, the Haidas were ready to sue for peace. From the shelter of the woods they maintained a hot but ineffective fire. Only one sailor was struck, suffering a flesh wound to one of his legs.

At last Chief Jefferson came off in a canoe, waving a white flag. He was followed by other leading Indians. Magistrate Franklyn instituted an inquiry, after which he placed Jefferson and four of his sub-chiefs under arrest. They were charged with piracy.

On arrival at Victoria the prisoners were lodged in jail where they remained for some weeks. In the meantime the police probed into the circumstances surrounding the attack on the schooner. When they discovered that the whisky had been salted their sympathies were aroused. The unofficial opinion was that any white man who would play such a trick, even on an Indian, deserved all that he got. As a consequence the charge of piracy was dropped. Chief Jefferson and his fellows promised to be good in future and were set free.

CHAPTER FOURTEEN

The Defiance of Ot-chee-wun

Chief Ot-chee-wun had only contempt for the whites. His Lamalchi warriors in their great canoes stalked unsuspecting settlers among the peaceful Gulf Islands — and boasted of the number they killed.

Lamalchi Bay, Kuper Island, is a pleasant place. There is nothing to indicate that it was once the home of a dreaded band of piratical Indians that required the entire resources of the North Pacific fleet to disperse them.

In 1863 Ot-chee-wun was a proud and haughty chief. His rule over the Lamalchi warriors was unquestioned. They were a fierce and resourceful tribe who were frequently at war with the Penelakuts, another Cowichan tribe that shared the island with them. From their lair they kept watch upon canoes and other craft in Stuart and Trincomali Channels and exacted such tribute as circumstances permitted. This form of piracy was not confined to the canoes of natives. Many white men and their boats vanished in the labyrinth of waters about the Gulf Islands and only Lamalchi braves could tell what had happened to them. For six years this robbery and murder had gone on. Ot-chee-wun had grown bold and contemptuous of the white man's law.

Ot-chee-wun was clever. He knew that sooner or later Governor James Douglas would strike back at him so he constructed a big blockhouse of heavy logs and loop-holed it for muskets. It was fully as strong as one of the bastions that had guarded the angles of Fort Victoria. He also had rifle pits dug at the entrance to the bay. When these fortifications were completed, Ot-chee-wun was confident that he could resist any white warriors who might come in their smoke-belching canoes. He was soon to have the opportunity.

On April 5, 1863, Bill Brady and a colored companion, John

83

Henlee, were attacked by Quamichans on a small island in Bedwell Harbour. Brady was killed and his companion, although wounded, managed to escape and reach Victoria. His arrival created much excitement that had not subsided before news of another atrocity added to public indignation. Frederick Marks, a settler, was moving his family from Miners Bay on Mayne Island to a new home on Waldron Island. He was in a boat with his married daughter, Caroline Harvey, while Mrs. Marks and several small children were being conveyed by Chris Mayer, a friend. The boats became separated. Marks decided to camp for the night on a small island off Saturna.

A canoe containing Lamalchi Indians sighted the white man's boat and stalked it along the shore line. When Marks and Mrs. Harvey landed at what appeared to be a suitable camping place the Indians watched from the nearby woods. When the settler stooped to light a fire the Indians shot him. Mrs. Harvey ran along the beach, but was pursued and captured. Then while one Indian held her, another killed her with an axe. Both bodies were weighted with stones and sunk in the sea.

Governor James Douglas determined that prompt measures should be taken to apprehend the killers. He asked Commodore John W.S. Spencer, officer in command of the North Pacific naval squadron at Esquimalt, for assistance in arresting those guilty of the murders. The Commodore assured the Governor that the navy would support the civil power to the limit.

HMS *Forward* was ordered to proceed to the Gulf Islands to investigate the reported atrocities. A start was made by instituting a search for Brady's body. The hunt for information commenced at Piers Island, then continued from island to island. In his quest for information about Brady, Lieutenant-Commander the Honorable Horace D. Lascelles, captain of the *Forward,* obtained some definite clues to the identity of the slayers of Marks and his daughter.

"I proceeded to Kuper Island with a view of arresting several Indians," stated the *Forward's* captain on his return to Victoria. "As they had declared their intention of resisting any attempt to arrest them, I had the rifle plates up, and the men's bags put in the intervening spaces. On arriving at the place, I found that they had a strong log house in the centre of the village, loop-holed. I then sent a message on shore by a canoe to say that I wished to speak to the chief, who returned an answer that he would not come, nor would he give up the murderers. I told them, through the interpreter . . . if the chief was not on board before the flag which we hoisted was hauled down, giving them a quarter of an hour, I would fire on the village."

But Ot-chee-wun was not frightened. He was confident in the strength of his fortifications. He knew, too, that while he waited for the flag to signal the start of battle, his marksmen in the rifle pits at both points of entrance to the bay were preparing to pick off any man aboard the *Forward* who showed himself.

"The chief answered that he would not come and he was not

Ot-chee-wun boasted that he had killed eleven whites and a number of Indians. He was described by the *Victoria Colonist* as "... a perfect fiend and the terror of all the tribes."

Whites in their rowboats, above, and Indians in their canoes, below, were especially vulnerable, as were settlers on isolated farms such as the one opposite on Saltspring Island.

afraid of us," Lascelles wrote. "At the end of the appointed time I hauled down the flag and fired into the village, which they deserted immediately and opened a very sharp fire of musketry from the two points at the entrance of the bay. I regret to say that one boy, Charles F. Glidden, was killed, being shot through the head whilst acting as powder-man at the pivot gun. Though the boat was hit in several places we sustained no other injury. The firing lasted about half an hour, when having thrown a few shells into the woods and knocked the village down, as much as possible, I went to Chemainus Bay for the night.

"The following morning I returned to Village Bay (the old name for Lamalchi Bay) and found that most of the Indians had left in the night. I completed the destruction of the village with a few shot and shell and returned to Cowichan."

Lascelles declared that the Lamalchis "are the terrors of the Coast to both Indians and white men, and make a boast of the number of white men they have killed."

Reinforcements arrived to extend the operations. Commodore Spencer sent HMS *Devastation*, Commander J.W. Pike; HMS *Cameleon*, Commander E. Hardinge; HMS *Grappler*, Lieutenant-Commander E.H. Verney, and two launches from HMS *Topaze*, with

The jail in Victoria where in 1863 Ot-chee-wun and three others were hanged for murdering white settlers.

sixty seamen and marines under Lieutenants Pusey and Geneste. In addition, the civil authorities sent Police Superintendent Horace Smith with a party of the Victoria Voltigeurs, the local militia unit. Such a formidable force had never before been used in a serious operation on the Pacific Coast.

An intensive search was begun for Ot-chee-wun and his immediate retinue. Warships patrolled the channels, boat crews examined every Indian village, and the Voltigeurs searched where every rumor said that the fugitives had been seen. By day and by night the hunt was prosecuted. Now it would center about Montague Harbour; next Osborne Bay would be the scene of activity; then Oyster Harbour would be carefully inspected. Word was brought that Ot-chee-wun had taken refuge in a mountain cave near the Chemainus River. Smith and his men forced their way through the thickets and combed the mountains, coming out at Cowichan Bay.

One by one Ot-chee-wun's relatives were located and seized as hostages. First his father-in-law, then his uncle, and his wife fell into the law's net. Day after day the man-hunt intensified, restricting the avenues of escape.

Nearly three weeks after the fight at Lamalchi Bay Commander Hardinge reported to Commodore Spencer that during the night sounds of musketry were heard near Montague Harbour on Galiano Island. At daylight he sent armed boats ashore to investigate.

"Shortly afterwards," he related, "Ot-chee-wun the chief pirate, and Shee-na-se-luk, his brother, were brought on board to our great satisfaction, their capture having been effected chiefly by the scouts tracking them closely, assisted by the Voltigeurs and by the number of men at Mr. Smith's disposal by which he was able to surround them and close all outlets of escape. In an hour after, the third man was captured, together with his wife and children. This was Wall-a-shuk."

The scouts who had finally run Ot-chee-wun to earth were mostly Penelakuts, who shared Kuper Island with the Lamalchis. They had their revenge for many an insult in the days of Ot-chee-wun's power and grandeur. Now the Lamalchi arrogance was humbled, the tribe was broken and impoverished, and all because Ot-chee-wun had defied the laws and authority of the Great White Queen.

The last act in the drama was set in the Assize Court at Victoria. Here Ot-chee-wun and three others went on trial for killing Marks, his daughter, and the seaman aboard HMS *Forward*. They were found guilty and hanged in the Colonial Jail yard at Victoria, July 4, 1863, with members of their tribe as witnesses.

CHAPTER FIFTEEN

The Chilcotin War

Early in the summer of 1864 Chilcotin warriors attacked the seventeen peaceful road builders, killing fourteen. It was the beginning of three months of murder and terror in the vast Chilcotin between the Fraser River and the Coast Mountains.

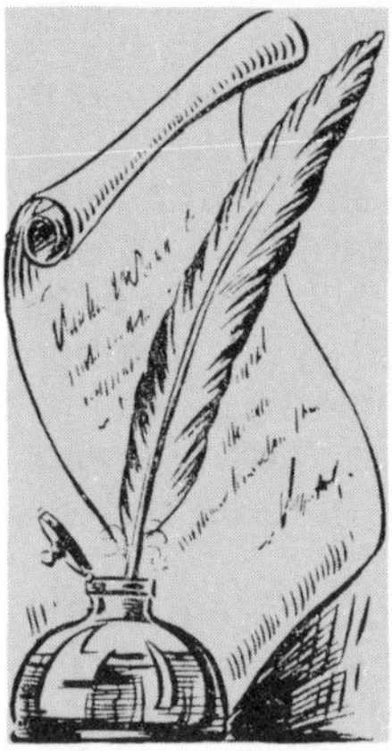

Massacre and terror cleared the vast 600-mile-wide territory between the Fraser River and the sea of its white population in 1864. The powerful Chilcotin tribe was on the warpath, pillaging and destroying. They were only subdued after an exhaustive three-month campaign by forces organized by Governor Frederick Seymour of the Crown Colony of British Columbia.

The real cause of the uprising and initial massacre of fourteen workers on the Bute Inlet road will never be known, but all accounts agree that the retirement of Sir James Douglas, as governor, was a contributing factor. The Indians did not understand how a great chief could be superseded in office. But of all the reasons suggested the most probable was the thoughtless act of an unnamed white man, who was said to have threatened some Chilcotins with the scourge of smallpox. When later he wrote their names — or pretended to — on paper, they were sure he was manufacturing a black spell, for the mysteries of reading and writing fascinated and frightened the natives.

Alfred Waddington, an educated and progressive business man of Victoria, planned the construction of a toll road from Bute Inlet to the goldfields of Cariboo. He was granted permission by the Government of the Crown Colony of British Columbia in 1862 and made a start on the work shortly after obtaining his charter. He found, however, that in addition to the natural obstacles of the country, progress promised to be impeded and endangered as a result of the ancient enmity between the Indians on the Coast and the Chilcotins. In 1844 the stealthy plainsmen had crossed the mountains and fallen upon a sleeping village on the banks of the Homathko River. Nineteen men and women had been butchered. Waddington determined to overcome the inter-tribal hatred that such acts of barbarity had engendered. He was successful and brought the Chilcotins and Coastal Indians together — in peace — and sealed the fate of his workers and his enterprise.

In 1863 there was harmony between the tribes and for the first time in generations the Chilcotins came through to tide-water without molestation. They engaged with Mr. Brewster, the superintendent of the construction crews, as packers and laborers. When the season's work was finished and the rough road had been pushed nearly forty miles up the rugged valley of the Homathko, the whites bartered their guns and ammunition to their Indian friends.

Such was the harmony that existed between them and the Chilcotins the previous season that when the whites returned to continue the work in the spring of 1864, they came unarmed. Brewster and his force of sixteen men had only one rifle and one revolver. They set no guards at night, an oversight that would have disastrous consequences.

Thirty miles up the river and some eight below the first and main camp, a ferry was operated by the current. Tim Smith managed the scow that the stream forced back and forth and also acted as storekeeper of the supply depot maintained at that point.

In April the Chilcotins reappeared. They were headed by Chief Klatsassin and Chiefs Tellot and Tappet, and included such noted warriors as Chassis and Piem, the former being described as of "fiendish visage." They appeared to be very friendly. Brewster and his men welcomed them as old friends and were in no way suspicious.

On the night of April 30 the Chilcotins struck. Tim Smith, at the ferry, was the first victim, being shot to death. The stores were pillaged and the ferry destroyed. The following morning as the first streaks of dawn fingered down the mountain into the darkened valleys, the murderous warriors fell upon the tents of the white men. By strange coincidence the camp had been built upon the very site where, two decades before, the Homathko village had been wiped out by Chilcotin raiders. In the absence of guards, the surprise was complete. The Indians crept close and cut the guy ropes of the tents. As the aroused men struggled beneath the canvas, the savages shot them and, to complete their barbarity, stabbed again and again through the cloth.

Brewster and three others were encamped in an advanced position two miles higher up the river. They were just about to start work when the Indians arrived. They were shot down. Only three men, two of them badly wounded, escaped alive out of seventeen comprising Waddington's road builders.

Indignation flamed high in both Crown Colonies, British

Alfred Waddington, whose hopes of building a toll road from Bute Inlet to the Cariboo died when fourteen of his seventeen men were murdered.

Opposite page: Part of Waddington's road along the rugged rock walls of the Homathco River, with the glacial peaks of the Coast Mountains in the background.

Donald McLean, opposite, was killed while pursuing the Chilcotins. A retired HBC trader, he had in 1849 participated in the murder of several Indians. He thereafter wore a breastplate which twice had saved him from bullets aimed at his heart. In the Chilcotin chase, however, he was shot in the back.

Opposite page: The trenches dug by the ill-fated Alexander McDonald and his packers are just up the hill from today's Stop-of-Interest sign shown on the inside front cover.
As long as the men stayed in the trenches they were able to beat off the Indian attacks. When they left, McDonald and two of his men were killed.

Columbia and Vancouver's Island, when word of the massacre was received. Outraged residents insisted that immediate steps be taken to punish the murderers. Although Governor Frederick Seymour was a new-comer to the Colony of British Columbia, he did not require experience to know what an Indian war would mean, or that neglect to avenge this massacre at Bute Inlet might start a general conflict. Seymour promptly ordered Police Inspector Chartres Brew to recruit a force and proceed to Bute Inlet and to arrest the Indians responsible, even if he had to follow them into the Interior of the Colony.

Brew and his men were transported up the coast by HMS *Forward.* They made their way up the Homathko with great difficulty, facing unexpected problems of transportation. At the ferry they found a scene of death and desolation. At the other places the bodies of the victims of the Chilcotins fury were found where they had fallen, and interred there. Brew and Thomas Elwyn, as justices of the peace, held an inquest.

Brew found it impossible to follow the Indians into their country from Bute Inlet since horses could not be driven through the mountains. He returned to New Westminster and told of the physical barriers that existed in the pathway of any attempt to force entry into the Interior. He was willing, if the Governor so desired, to endeavor to get through, but he thought another route would be more feasible.

The Governor agreed and after some discussion it was decided to try the Palmer Trail from Bella Coola. At the same time orders were sent to Gold Commissioner William Cox in the neighboring Cariboo to raise a force and proceed into the Chilcotin to join the party under Brew from the Coast. Cox soon had an armed party of sixty-eight men under his command. Donald McLean, former Hudson's Bay Company official, went along as his lieutenant. McLean knew the country well and was acquainted with the Indians.

Brew's force was smaller, but was for the most part composed of disciplined soldiers for he recruited a number of men from the disbanded Royal Engineers corps, while the remainder of his men were carefully selected. The unit comprised thirty-eight rank and file. Governor Seymour decided to accompany this party, while Lieutenant Cooper, of the Royal Marines, also went along. Some valuable strength was obtained at Bella Coola when a friendly chief of that tribe volunteered to join the force with a number of his men. They had some old scores to settle with the Chilcotins.

While these preparations were being made Klatsassin and his braves were strewing the Chilcotin plains with death and destruction. A settler named William Manning, a quiet inoffensive man who had no quarrel with the Indians and who was developing a piece of land near Puntzi Lake, was picked out for assassination. Klatsassin sent him word that he must die — for no other reason than that he was a white man. The message was followed quickly by the Indian executioners. Manning offered no resistance and was shot down in cold blood.

"Manning was the only fixed settler in the country" commented Governor Seymour later in recounting the story of the Chilcotin War, "but unfortunately a train of horses with eight drivers was approaching from Bentinck Arm . . . Klatsassin went to meet them and, as in the case of Manning, told McDonald, the head of the party, he had come to put them all to death.

"But," continued the Governor, "the eight men were well armed, showed they were likely to sell their lives dearly, and the Indians hesitated and then apparently retired. But McDonald knew they were not far off and threw up some earthworks on the summit of a small hill and remained in safety for some days. Then he determined on retreating as far as he could to the Bella Coola country. As his party left their shelter the Chilcotins approached in force and galloped towards him. The white men were first to reach a long, narrow Indian bridge over a swamp, which they were well able to hold against the natives, who again retired, but only to form an ambush on the trail. A volley was then fired at the train as it passed. Two of the men were dismounted, a horse killed, and then an open attack was made by an overwhelming force . . . McDonald and two of his party were killed. The fortunate accident of the horses running between the Indians and the packers enabled five of the latter to escape, though three were badly wounded."

Intoxicated with success, the Chilcotins raided down into the valley of the Bella Coola in hopes of killing a settler named Hamilton. He was forewarned and, with his wife and daughter, escaped down the river.

Cox's party from Cariboo reached Puntzi Lake, but through lack of caution in approaching, alarmed Klatsassin's band which might have been surprised and defeated. The Indians prepared to attack at the first opportunity. Cox, alarmed at the situation, hastily constructed a log fort on top of a small hill. Here he was when Brew's force found him, "besieged by an invisible foe," Seymour sneered.

The little force from the Coast, under Brew, had pushed rapidly into the Interior. They expected to be attacked at a landmark called the "Big Slide" and could not understand why the Chilcotins had not taken the opportunity offered by the terrain at that point. They advanced steadily towards the place appointed for the rendezvous with the Cariboo contingent. This was in the country of Chief Anaheim, a noted chief, who was suspected of giving support to Klatsassin. Brew and the Governor were both anxious to bring this chief in to camp. Lieutenant Cooper, with a "flying force" was sent in search of him. They chased him right up to the snow crest of the mountains and only desisted in pursuit when faced by starvation.

The Governor was disgusted when he found Cox idling behind the walls of his log fort instead of chasing Indians. He ordered Cox to pursue Klatsassin, reported to be heading towards the difficult mountainous country at the head of Bute Inlet. This duty was accepted willingly since it was more a lack of direction than of courage that had held the miners at Puntzi Lake.

The Governor was anxious to contact Chief Alexis, another powerful leader of the Chilcotins, to prevent him from identifying himself openly with the insurrection. At last, through promise of immunity, Alexis agreed to meet the Governor. The arrival of the chief for the conference was graphically described by Seymour:

"Forming his men into some sort of order on the plain, Alexis and his men came on at the best pace of their horses, holding their muskets over their heads to show they came in peace. Having ascertained which was the Governor, he threw himself from his horse and at once approached me. He was dressed in a French uniform, such as one sees in pictures of Montcalm."

Cox and his Cariboo Volunteers made rapid progress towards

Judge Matthew Baillie Begbie, left, Police Inspector Chartres Brew, and Quesnel in the early 1860s. Klatsassin and the other Chilcotins were buried on the bank of the Fraser River at the far end of the street.

Chilco Lake, the hunting and fishing grounds of the Chilcotins under Klatsassin. On the way, however, they were ambushed near Choelquoit Lake. Donald McLean was shot through the heart as he scouted ahead of the main body. Cox, deprived of the experienced McLean, at once retreated to Puntzi Lake and the wrath of Seymour. The Governor asked Brew, with his smaller force, to pursue the fugitives. This duty was accepted without demur, although the New Westminster contingent was desperately short of supplies. A pack train from the Coast was expected, but it had not arrived and some fears were entertained for its safety.

Brew and his men made all possible haste towards the Chilco Lake region and into the heart of the mountains. They faced not only the difficulties and dangers of mountain warfare, but the spectre of starvation. Relentlessly they followed Klatsassin and his warriors, moving with such rapidity that the Indians had no time to fish or hunt. Brew was beating them at their own style of warfare. At last the chief broke from the hills and led his men back to the plains. Here he found that Cox's force barred his advance to the north and east. On August 15 near the old Hudson's Bay Company fort on the Chilcotin River he surrendered.

"I have brought seven murderers and I am one myself," Klatsassin announced in giving himself up. "I return to you one horse and one mule and twenty dollars for the Government as a token of good faith. The names of those present are, myself, Tellot, Cheeloot, Tappet, Piem, Chassis, Chaddiki, Sanstanki. There are ten more at large. These men, I know, cannot be caught before early spring, when they come out to the lake for sustenance. Three others are dead; one was killed by McDonald, the other two killed themselves. There was altogether twenty-one Indians implicated in the massacre."

Such was Klatsassin's confession, but there were many more Indians involved than the butchers of the Homathko Valley. Governor Seymour had no illusions as to the real character of the affair. "It suited our purpose to treat officially these successive acts of violence as isolated massacres," he confided to the Colonial Secretary in London, "but there is no objection to our now avowing that an Indian insurrection existed."

No effort was made to apprehend the remaining ten accused by Klatsassin of having a part in the slaughtering of the road workers. It has proved too difficult and expensive to capture those who had been brought to trial and it was considered that the execution of the five would prove to be an effective lesson to all Chilcotins.

Klatsassin and his gang of murderers were taken to Quesnel where they came before stern-faced Justice Matthew Baillie Begbie and jury. Five were found guilty — Klatsassin, and his fellow chiefs, Tellot and Tappet, and two braves, Piem and Chassis, the Ugly One. On a cold October morning they paid for their crimes on the scaffold. The Chilcotin War was over.

CHAPTER SIXTEEN

The Pirates of Clayoquot

Warriors of the Ahousat tribe brutally murdered then mutilated the bodies of the two white traders and their Indian helper. But because of a ruling by Vancouver Island's Justice David Cameron the culprits went unpunished.

Heathenism protected piracy and saved a number of West Coast Indians from possible death on the scaffold. The British Navy was thwarted by a legal technicality and brutal murder went unpunished when, in 1864, the Supreme Court of Vancouver's Island refused to hear unsupported Indian testimony.

It was in the summer of that year that Captain George Stevenson took his sloop *Kingfisher* to Clayoquot Sound on a trading cruise. He was assisted by a powerful young man named Wilson and a Fort Rupert Indian. He had a more or less successful stay in the Sound and was on the point of leaving when he was hailed by an Ahousat Indian who told him that he had a large quantity of fish oil to trade. Stevenson decided to stay another day and ran the sloop in to anchorage at the mouth of Matilda Creek.

Next morning, according to official records, Chief Cap-chah of the Ahousat tribe with ten or a dozen of his fighting men boarded the 16-ton craft. Without warning Stevenson was stabbed to death. Wilson, the mate, fought fiercely but was finally seized by four or five Indians. He was held down on the deck while another savage plunged a dagger into his chest. The Fort Rupert Indian was taken prisoner, held for several days, then beheaded with an axe. The bodies were mutilated and sunk in the sea, the cargo pillaged and the sloop scuttled.

Rumor of this act of piracy reached Victoria and HMS *Devastation,* Commander J.W. Pike, was sent to make inquiries. The Indians prepared for war and Chief Cedar-Canim, who was friendly to the whites, warned the warship's captain to proceed cautiously. Superintendent of Police Horace Smith, L.B. Lewis, a colored man from Chemainus who had a flair for solving murder mysteries, and an Indian interpreter was taken along. In addition to the *Kingfisher* murders, a pioneer trader named William Banfield, had also been killed, and the police official was anxious to have this case cleared up.

When the *Devastation* reached Clayoquot Sound, Commander Pike sent two boats towards shore to make contact with the Indians. Before they could land, however, they were surrounded by a fleet of war canoes. The painted warriors boldly proclaimed their lack of fear and in a scuffle that ensued bruised Dr. Gregory, the surgeon of the *Devastation,* and tore off most of his clothes.

The *Devastation* returned to Victoria and Commander Pike reported the attitude of the Indians to Rear Admiral Joseph Denman. That bluff old sea-dog could hardly believe that savages would dare to challenge the might and authority of the British Navy. There must be some mistake. He would go and see for himself. He ordered his flagship HMS *Sutlej* to proceed to Clayoquot, with the *Devastation* to follow. He again gave permission to Police Superintendent Smith to accompany the navy, while Philip J. Hankin from the Colonial Secretary's office and his interpreter, "Friday," were also civil representatives.

The Ahousat villages at Matilda Creek and Bawden Bay were deserted when the warships arrived. The *Sutlej* went up the North Arm of Clayoquot to a village named Sik-tok-kis where a native, En-qui-ok-chittle, said to have been implicated in the attack on the *Kingfisher,* was captured. He admitted having witnessed the slaughter on the sloop and gave a detailed account of the killing of Stevenson and Wilson.

While the *Sutlej* was visiting Sik-tok-kis, the *Devastation* went up Herbert Arm to the village of Moo-yah-kah where three of the alleged pirates were reported to be hiding. The Indians opened fire on the boats from the warship. This defiance was reported to the Admiral and he ordered the *Devastation* to proceed to the North Arm villages, while the *Sutlej* would take a look at the Indians of Moo-yah-kah. The *Devastation* destroyed Sik-tok-kis and several other native encampments in Shelter Arm. At each place loot from the *Kingfisher* was found.

"I sent Friday into Moo-yah-hak under the ship's guns," the Admiral told Governor Kennedy of Vancouver's Island on his return. "A number of Indians came down and had a palaver with him on the beach; he told them I promised not to fire upon them if they delivered up to me all the men concerned in the affair of the *Kingfisher,* three of whom I knew to be there. Friday, on his return, brought a message from the Indians saying that if I wanted the men I might come and take them; if I destroyed the village they would build it up again, and if I attempted to touch the canoes they would shoot every man who came near the shore.

Rear Admiral Joseph Denman, above, was incensed when Vancouver Island's Chief Justice David Cameron, at right above, ruled that two natives suspected of murder could not be placed on trial since they were heathens. The pirates of Clayoquot went free — and Chief Justice Cameron was retired soon after.

An 1864 on-the-scene drawing of boats from HMS *Devastation* and *Sutlej* attacking native villages in Clayoquot Sound with rockets.
The top photos show HMS *Sutlej* and her gun deck. The warship's cannon were used to bombard the natives at Clayoquot.

"I then ordered a heavy fire to be opened on the village and on the surrounding bush to clear it and sent in the gigs to complete the destruction of the village under cover of the ship's guns and those of the heavy boats. Notwithstanding these precautions several musket shots were fired at the boats but were instantly silenced by the boats' guns, which replied with admirable precision."

Having completely destroyed the big village of Moo-yah-kah, the *Sutlej* steamed back to Matilda Creek, bringing a dozen canoes with her. Orders were given Commander Pike to destroy Capchah's big village at Cypress Bay. "Here," said Commander Pike in his log book, "the natives made a regular stand, and fired upon the boats, but luckily no lives were lost. Destroyed and burnt the entire ranch. Proceeded still further up to the head of Bedwell Sound and found another village. Captured and destroyed 22 canoes and burnt the village. The natives fired upon us here."

Thus the search went on. Villages were bombarded and burned, salmon weirs destroyed and fine cedar canoes smashed — but still the wily Cap-chah evaded capture. Now Admiral Denman determined to fight the Indians on shore and in their own style of warfare, by surprise. He landed a force of twenty sailors and forty marines, and a few friendly Indians under command of Senior Lieutenant High Stewart of the *Sutlej*. Smith, Hankin and Friday accompanied the expedition. They were to make their way from White Cove, Herbert Arm, through the woods and attack Cap-chah's home village on Trout River.

It was a most difficult task, Lieutenant Stewart later reported, "to make progress through the swamps and tangled underbrush." Finally the attacking force reached the approaches to the village. Lieutenant J.W. Maxwell, with the sailors, was left in ambush to prevent the Indians escaping across the ford of Trout River. Just as the marines were about to open attack, a number of dogs detected the white men and set up a tremendous barking. The Indians who had been busy repairing old canoes and other tasks dropped their work, seized their weapons and disappeared into the woods.

Now the battle commenced. The Ahousats opened a brisk fire on that part of the bush where their dogs indicated the marines were under cover. The trained soldiers returned the fire with a degree of coolness and effectiveness that won high praise from their commander. The fighting continued for half an hour, during which time not a single white man was hit, but at least ten Indians were killed and others wounded.

The Admiral, not wishing to continue a campaign that was so destructive, determined to return to Victoria with his single prisoner. He obtained a witness who was ready to give evidence of piracy of the Ahousats. Before leaving, however, he gave solemn warning to the Indians of Clayoquot that he would return in a month and if the others accused of taking part in the murders on board the sloop were not surrendered at that time he would bombard other villages.

They now knew what the threat implied, for nine of their rancheries had been shattered, many had been killed and sixty-four canoes demolished.

The Ahousat and another Indian who was suspected of being implicated in the murder of Banfield were placed on trial in the Supreme Court before Mr. Justice David Cameron. The aging jurist ascertained that neither native was a Christian and that the Indian witnesses were also heathens. Sadly he shook his head and sighed; "These people do not believe in the existence of a Supreme Being and therefore they are not competent to take an oath." Such being his belief, he could not accept the evidence that they might give. The officials were dumbfounded, but Admiral Denman was not; he was indignantly vocal.

"From the refusal to admit Indian testimony," the angry admiral told Governor Kennedy, "it follows that as long as the Natives, in attacks upon British traders, take care to leave no survivors to give evidence they are perfectly secure from conviction and punishment in the Supreme Court at Victoria."

The Admiral was in an unfortunate position, as he pointed out to the Governor. If he went after the murderers again it was with the fore-knowledge they would be liberated if arrested; if he did not keep his promise of returning to Clayoquot the Indians would lose faith in the word of the Navy. Nevertheless, the Governor would not permit him to continue the hunt for the slayers of the *Kingfisher's* crew and the pirates of Clayoquot went free.

The Admiral believed that the action of the court would be misinterpreted by the Indians and endanger white traders. It would appear from subsequent events on the coast that there was some justification for this fear. It is hard to understand the reason for Justice Cameron's ruling, as the previous year he had hanged an Indian upon testimony of another native.

The Admiral was undoubtedly heartened, however, by a later development. Not long after his rejection of Indian testimony, Mr. Justice Cameron was retired.

The Obstinacy of Chief Jim

Even though guns of a British warship destroyed his village, canoes and food supplies, Chief Jim won the quiet admiration of Colonial officials when he stubbornly refused to surrender three of his tribe accused of murder.

It was not usual, in early Colonial days, for the authorities to interfere in purely inter-tribal disputes among the native nations, or to take official notice of killings that resulted from the bitter feuds that swayed communities in the carrying out of the age-old blood code of the Coast. Efforts of the white governments at Victoria and New Westminster were mainly directed towards providing safety for the traders and travellers who visited the more remote localities along the jagged coastline.

It was just a few days before Christmas, 1865, when HMS *Clio,* Captain N.E.B. Turnour, dropped anchor off Fort Rupert near the northern end of Vancouver's Island. She had been on a cruise up the coast in an endeavor to put a stop to whisky peddling, as well as to investigate other reported illegalities. The ship had encountered rough weather and it was with some difficulty that Captain Alex. J. Chambers, the civilian pilot, found the entrance to Bate Passage on the way to the Hudson's Bay Company's fort.

Although it was late at night when the warship finally anchored in Beaver Harbour, it was not too late for Pym N. Compton, officer in charge, to come on board with a tale of woe. His Chinese cook, whose wizardry with foods Captain Turnour had experienced on his way north, had committed suicide after confessing that he had murdered several men in Cariboo whose ghosts now impelled him to hang himself. There was another, more serious, development that Compton related to the captain. It was that a Nahwitti Indian, from the band at the northern end of the Island, had been murdered by three Fort Rupert Indians.

The Indians residing in the vicinity of the post were fearless. Originally they had dwelt across Milbanke Sound near Fort McLoughlin, but when the post was abandoned and Fort Rupert later constructed they had followed the white traders. They were ruled by Chief Jim, a bold and aggressive individual, who, with his warriors, was becoming insolent and contemptuous of the occupants of the fort. This attitude, it was believed, was largely due to the failure of the authorities to bring to justice the perpetrators of several massacres of the crews of coastal trading schooners. Not since the Nahwitti villages were blasted by warships in 1850-51 for the killing of several sailors had threatened punishment fallen upon native rancheries in that locality, although warnings of disciplinary action had been voiced on several occasions. This growing contempt for the white men had even brought suggestions that the stockades might be scaled and Fort Rupert easily captured, with consequent distribution of the treasures in trade goods stored there.

Captain Turnour, after hearing the story of the murder, decided to take action. Chief Jim must be taught that the power of the Queen's navy was greater than the valor and assembled strength of an Indian tribe. So the next morning First Lieutenant C.J. Carey was ordered to land with a strong party and demand the surrender of the killers of the Nahwitti.

Here is the terse, but eloquent report of Lieutenant Carey:

"On Friday the 22nd of December, I landed at Fort Rupert, by the order of Captain Turnour, to demand the persons of 3 Indians who had murdered an Indian from Nahwitti, as well as to search the village for whiskey.

"On landing I was met on the beach by 'Jim' the Chief of the Tribe, who asked for what purpose we had landed. I told him to secure the 3 murderers, and destroy any whiskey we might find. He refused to give the Natives up, unless we gave him 2 of our men as hostages; during that time about 50 Indians assembled on the beach, and about the same number near the Ranch, armed with muskets, they commenced yelling, and fired in the air over our heads.

" 'Jim', the chief, was evidently the prime mover; he appeared to be urging his men to fire on us, and was very threatening in his manner. I told him he should have a certain time to give the men up, and if they were not then forth-coming, we would open fire from the ship and destroy the village. At the expiration of the time appointed we fired upon the Ranch, and totally destroyed it, with 50 or 60 large canoes. We then made a prisoner of Jim and 10 other of the Natives."

A full account of what occurred that day and subsequently was told by Captain Chambers in a report published in *The British Colonist,* January 5 and 6, 1866. Chief Jim, the pilot said, announced that he and his men would attack the fort as soon as the warship

The village of Nahwitti in 1881. Murder of a Nahwitti Indian by three Fort Rupert Indians resulted in Chief Jim refusing to surrender the culprits — with drastic consequences to his people.

had departed, in retaliation for the bombardment.

While explosives were bursting in the wooden houses, sending cedar boards splintering in the air, the Indians took refuge behind the fort where shot from the *Clio* could not reach them.

Before returning to the ship, Lieutenant Carey directed a force of marines to reinforce the little garrison of Company employees in the fort. Here they could help to man the palisades and operate the guns in the bastions in the event of an attempt by the natives to take the place. He gave the marines strict orders not to start trouble, but to act on the defensive.

In describing the affair, Captain Chambers said: "After some rounds, the Indians gave in, hauling down four flags which they had defiantly raised, and hoisting a white flag in their place; but though Mr. Compton urged them to give up the three murderers, they refused. The *Clio* hauled off again to a more suitable berth for the night."

Chief Jim was a prisoner but he had won the first round for he persisted in his refusal to surrender the wanted men. Chambers could not help admiring the courage of the Indians: "We learned that a man and his wife were severely contused by the bursting of a shell in one of the houses," he said. "I saw a shot strike close to the man who was raising the white flag, but he appeared as unconcerned as possible, neither looking to the right or left."

Captain Chambers stayed all night at the fort where everyone was kept on the alert by Indians whooping and yelling and knocking at the gate. They were trying to induce the defenders to sally out. Failing in that ruse, they offered to surrender the men if a party went out to take them in charge. Their object was to secure hostages. Compton recognized the purpose of the natives and refused to fall into the obvious trap. Throughout the long hours of darkness the Indians buried the food supplies in the houses that remained standing and dug hiding places in the dry earthern floors of the structures that had been demolished by the bombardment.

In vain did Compton and Morris Moss, an Indian agent for the Crown Colony of British Columbia who was favorably known to the Fort Ruperts, try to get the chiefs to agree to the demands of Captain Turnour. They were obdurate.

In the morning, Lieutenant Carey landed with another strong force of sailors and marines. He once more appealed to the natives to surrender the alleged killers. They refused, and Jim, in custody on the *Clio*, maintained his stubborn refusal to order his people to give the men to the naval officers. Lieutenant Carey told the Indians that unless his demand was met he would be compelled to complete the destruction of the village. The answer was a decided "No."

The torch was then applied to the shattered dwellings. Soon red flames were reaching into the wintry sky. A fire break halted the destruction when about half the village — and its valuable stores of winter food hidden a few inches deep in the earthern floors — had been destroyed.

Once more Lieutenant Carey, who was reluctant to inflict more suffering on the tribe, asked if they would not bend to the authority of the Queen's officer. They would not. Again the fire was kindled and soon the last of the fine big cedar community houses was blazing fiercely. When only hot embers remained to indicate to the homeless Fort Ruperts where the houses had been the identical demand for the guilty three to be produced met with the same determined refusal. On the warship Chief Jim, who stolidly watched the destruction of his encampment, scorned the repeated suggestion that he comply and save his people from further punishment and himself from the white man's jail.

When no more houses remained to be burned the chiefs were told that persistence in their obstinate course would bring destruction of all the canoes that had escaped the bombardment of the previous day. The canoe to the Coast Indian was of more importance than his house since it was his only means of travel and the vehicle in which he sought food from the sea. The Indians did not hesitate; they rejected the opportunity of saving the remainder of their fleet. The orders were given and the sailors and marines sadly went to work breaking up the cedar dug-outs. Every craft that could be found was broken. In all, Captain Turnour later reported, the Indians lost more than one hundred canoes.

There was nothing more that the captain of the *Clio* could do to force compliance with his demand, so he left for Victoria. He took Chief Jim and the others with him, not only to endeavor to bring him to reason in the environment of Victoria's jail, but as hostages to secure the safety of the fort.

The authorities of the Colony must have had a quiet admiration for the unfortunate chief, whose offense had been one of omission rather than commission. After holding him a short time he was liberated. He had established that his will was stronger than the might of the navy — but he had paid a terrible price in proving it. He also learned the hard way that the navy would and could back up its threats when occasion demanded.

CHAPTER EIGHTEEN

When Chief Isadore Ran Riot

When a Kootenay Indian named Kapla was arrested for murder, Chief Isadore and twenty-four braves with cocked Winchesters promptly released him. War between the isolated settlers and Isadore's 300 mounted warriors seemed imminent.

Close to the restored log buildings of the old North-West Mounted Police barracks at Fort Steele, where the Kootenay and St. Mary Rivers join, stands a memorial cairn. It recalls that Superintendent Sam Steele and officers and men of "B" Division of the famous force erected the "fort" in 1887, and their presence "secured peace and order in the country at a critical time."

From musty government files at Victoria, official reports and records of the Dominion, and news stories of the time something of the tense drama in East Kootenay may be glimpsed. Only two years before Louis Riel had induced Big Bear and other Indian chiefs on the plains to rise in rebellion. The memory of the massacre at Frog Lake (See Frontier book, *Frog Lake Massacre*) and the long expensive campaign that was required to subdue the rebels justified the nervousness of the authorities. While the plaque at Fort Steele properly recounts the founding of the North-West Mounted Police post in British Columbia, space prevented reference being made to the parts played by Dr. Israel W. Powell, Indian Commissioner; Magistrate A.W. Vowell and L.W. Herchmer, of the Mounted, who formed a commission to inquire into the reason why Chief Isadore and his people had threatened trouble. This commission succeeded in restoring peace before the arrival of Major Steele and his men.

Throughout the story runs the red trail of a double murder that remains unsolved to this day. It was one of the causes of dissatisfaction on the part of the Indians, for two members of Chief Isadore's tribe were suspected of the crime. A more fundamental cause, however, was the fear by the natives that slowly expanding settlement and land surveying presaged the extinction of tribal existence.

The Canadian Pacific Railway was being pushed through the Rocky Mountains in 1884 and 1885. Among the thousands of men employed were many crooks, gamblers and general ne'er-do-wells. They mostly entered from United States and travelled north from the border by the old trade trails to Wild Horse Creek, from there to the headwaters of the Columbia and down that river to Golden.

The British Columbia government was insufficiently provided with police to cope with the situation and for a time the Mounted Police kept order along the right-of-way. In the multi-thousand-square-mile territory extending south from the railway to the United States, and east from the Arrow Lakes to the Rockies — an area larger than many European countries — only two men represented law and order. One was Harry Anderson, constable, recorder and entrusted with all else that departments might require to be done. He was stationed at the old mining camp of Wild Horse Creek where he operated under "Judge" Vowell, as the Magistrate was known. Vowell, in turn, in matters concerning law and order, communicated with Deputy Attorney-General P. Irving, in Victoria some 600 miles and weeks of travel away.

Such was the situation when, in August 1885, Vowell reported that the previous year it became known that two miners had been murdered near Deadman's Creek, 52 miles south of Kicking Horse. These men were later identified as Hylton and Kemp, two experienced and respected prospectors.

When the Deputy Attorney-General at Victoria learned of the crime, he instructed Magistrate Vowell to use every endeavor to solve the mystery. His suspicion was that it was the work of Indians, but he advised that every possible clue should be followed. He wrote to Vowell saying that Magistrate Sproat, at Farwell, (Revelstoke) had heard a rumor that the deed might have been committed by the "Long Haired Man," who had been working on the grade but had left about the time that Hylton and Kemp disappeared.

Constable Anderson, at Wild Horse, was using every endeavor to unravel the mystery. Like Irving, he thought that the killings were the work of Indians, but he immediately started to investigate the suspicions aroused by Sproat's report. He went to Spokane, located the Long Haired Man and thoroughly satisfied himself that there was no ground for the rumor. Harry Anderson was a very busy man in a very large territory, but he gave every moment he could spare from his other important duties to the case. His interest was heightened by the fact that he knew Hylton some years before in Cariboo, while Kemp was a man who also bore a good reputation. After some weeks of careful and painstaking work he learned that Kemp was wearing a gold watch and carrying three valuable gold

Chief Isadore and his Council at Fort
Steele. When Isadore and his braves,
using their Winchesters as persuaders,
set free one of his men arrested as a
murder suspect, the isolated settlers
feared that armed conflict would erupt.

Little Isadore, above right, was one of
the suspects in the murder of the two
prospectors.

Special constable F.W. Aylmer, right, was
one of the two policemen forced to leave
Wildhorse Creek by Chief Isadore.

Left: Superintendent Sam B. Steele,
seated, and NWMP near Golden in 1885.
In 1887 Steele and some seventy-five
mounties were sent to the East Kootenay
to help settle the Isadore affair.

nuggets at the time of his death, and these valuables were missing. Further meticulous detective work revealed that the watch had been purchased from a Victoria jeweller who was able to supply the number. The watch and nuggets, he informed his superiors, would be necessary to identify the murderers. Every effort should be concentrated upon finding them.

A squaw informed Anderson that three Indians — Kapla, Little Isadore and a boy — seemed to be hiding something of value. These Indians had been avoiding the officer. "The only chance would be, should the three be arrested," Anderson wrote to Vowell, "that the boy be admitted to give Queen's evidence."

Not until March 1887, however, did an opportunity arise to arrest Kapla. Judge Vowell was at the Coast when the Attorney-General's department received a telegram from Donald, where Steve Redgrave was acting as Government agent during Vowell's absence. It relayed a message from Anderson, carried from Wild Horse Creek by R.T. Galbraith:

"Donald, 17th. March, 1887

"Reported to you from Anderson today — Arrested Kapla (suspected) murderer of Hylton — gaol broken open by 25 armed Indians headed by Isadore and prisoners released. Galbraith with despatch arrived today — Says lives of settlers in jeopardy — Prompt action necessary — Trail open to John's — Will forward letter.

"S. Redgrave."

A similar message was received direct from Galbraith. These wires caused great alarm in Government circles. Chief Isadore was a powerful chief who could put 300 mounted warriors armed with rifles into the field. Worse, several years before the Kootenays had been toying with the idea of warfare in which it was expected they would be joined by other tribes on both sides of the International Boundary.

Scattered settlers in the Kootenays were thrown into panic by the actions of the Indians. It looked as if this was the time of terror young braves had been hinting at when they were objecting to land surveys. A meeting of white men was hastily called and Isadore asked to attend. He did so, with some of his leading men. The chief dominated the gathering. He, himself, did not want trouble, he said — and there was reason to believe him. Isadore was a wealthy man amongst his people, his possessions, mainly horses, being valued at $20,000. But while he did not want trouble, the young men, he said, were in a dangerous mood.

This mood was evident from the fact that after Anderson placed Kapla under arrest about two dozen Indians armed with Winchester rifles had gone to the jail at Wild Horse Creek and demanded his release. Anderson had refused to liberate Kapla, Isadore declared. It was then that the Indians smashed their way into the jail and released the suspect. Now, Isadore went on, he wanted Mr. Anderson and Honorable F.W. Aylmer, a surveyor who had acted

A prospector and his dog outside his cabin in the East Kootenay, and the community of Wildhorse Creek in the 1880s. The murder of two prospectors in 1884 and the subsequent actions by Chief Isadore left East Kootenay residents fearing for their lives.

as one of the constables, sent out of the country. The settlers agreed to the chief's demand and asked the two men to leave the district until the natives had quietened down.

Attorney-General A.E.B. Davie, on receipt of the wire from Donald, conferred with Premier William Smithe, who telegraphed Sir John A. Macdonald at Ottawa, asking for a division of the Mounted Police. Before the preliminaries of such aid being extended by the Dominion to the province could be completed, the country was shocked by the sudden death of Premier Smithe. This development delayed action. In the meantime, Dr. Israel W. Powell, Superintendent of Indian Affairs, was in contact with Ottawa and agreed to head a commission, consisting of Magistrate Vowell and Assistant Commissioner L.W. Herchmer of the North-West Mounted Police, to inquire into the problem.

The Commission hastened to Kootenay where, Dr. Powell later reported, "immediately after our arrival, the Indians were summoned to meet the commission at the Government office, Wild Horse Creek. Chief Isadore and a full representation of his tribe attended. After making them a speech, in which the gravity of the crime of which they had been guilty was fully explained, the demands of the Government were explicitly defined. The Indians were then given three days to consider the conditions submitted to them."

The Kootenays held a grand council and, at the end of the three days, Isadore informed Dr. Powell that the conditions were accepted.

The community which grew up around Fort Steele died when bypassed by the railway. However, it is today being restored by the B.C. government and annually attracts tens of thousands of visitors. Above is one of the NWMP barrack buildings.

These included the return of Constables Anderson and Aylmer and the surrender of Kapla when required by the authorities. Chief Isadore and some of his leading men signed a bond guaranteeing good faith in adhering to the terms. In announcing the settlement Dr. Powell commented, "a feeling of perfect security now prevails throughout the district."

The Commissioners had assured the natives that consideration would be given to their complaints respecting their reserves and that the Honorable Peter O'Reilly, as special commissioner, would come to see them. Isadore, himself, was making claim to property owned by Colonel James Barker, land upon which the city of Cranbrook is now situated.

On June 28, 1887, some seventy-five men of the North-West Mounted Police under Superintendent Samuel B. Steele arrived at Golden. Here they stayed until July 17 when they started for the source of the Columbia, from where they would go to Wild Horse Creek. Supplies were to be carried by steamer as far as possible but the little sternwheeler *Duchess* tried to carry too big a load and capsized. The only other steamer on the river was much smaller. She was the *Clive*, so slow that she could not keep up with the mounted men riding along the stream bank. At last they reached Columbia Lake from where Galbraith's efficient pack trains carried the supplies the rest of the way.

The force arrived at Six Mile Creek, near Bummer's Flat, where it was intended to form an establishment. Closer examination revealed the location to be unsuitable, so Steele purchased ten acres from the Galbraiths where they operated a ferry across the Kootenay River. Here an extensive log fort was constructed, the buildings forming a square, and named Fort Steele.

Soon after his arrival Steele called upon Isadore to produce Kapla. True to his word, the Chief did. Little Isadore, the other suspect, was also surrendered, as was the boy. The youngster stubbornly refused to repeat stories of the killing of Hylton and Kemp that he was reported to have told. As Anderson had pointed out several years before, without the boy's story and the location of the watch and nuggets it was impossible to prove anything against any person in connection with the crime. The charges were dropped. The Mounted then undertook to solve the murder mystery, but a year later Superintendent Steele informed Ottawa that it was impossible.

When Commissioner O'Reilly arrived he could find no basis for Isadore's claim to Colonel Baker's land. The chief grew angry, but was mollified by equally good lands allotted to him at St. Mary. So ended the Kootenay "rebellion" scare that brought the Mounted Police into British Columbia to establish a fort. It caused a great deal of excitement while it lasted, and gave rise to fears that a general Indian war patterned after the North-West Rebellion of 1885 might break out. The matter could easily have been more serious had not both governments acted with promptness and courage.

Background Notes:

Chapter One:

Attack on the Atahualpa — Captain J.T. Walbran, in his monumental work, *British Columbia Coast Names* under the listing "Dryad Point" tells the story of the fight as he learned it from both native sources and from the pages of the "Annual Register for the Year 1806."

The Tonquin's Captain — A privately printed biographical sketch of Lieutenant Jonathan Thorn was written by his great grandson, Charles E. Thorn, of New York, in 1934. The pages of the brochure shed a more favorable light on his character. A man of "magnificent physique" he "was a thoroughly experienced naval officer and a skilled and practical navigator". He had served with distinction, under Decatur, in the war between United States and the pirates of the Barbary Coast. But Thorn was not suited to be a fur trader. He was bluff, straightforward and did not have "two prices".

The Deadly Insult — The family version of what started the massacre on the *Tonquin's* decks is that tiring of haggling with the Claquoquot chief, he abandoned "all further efforts to bargain with his shuffling customer, he thrust his hands in his pockets and paced up and down the deck in silence. The cunning old Indian followed him to and fro, holding out a sea otter skin to him at every turn and pestering him to trade." Then the Indian started to jeer at the white man and his low prices. The captain was in no mood for such treatment. "Turning suddenly, he snatched the proffered otter skin from his hands, rubbed it in his face and dismissed him over the side."

Chapter Two:

Surprise Attack — The effort on the part of the Haida Indians to capture the *Lady Washington* was told in a number of log books and journals of officers of trading vessels of the time. The story told by John Hoskins, clerk of the *Columbia,* and that penned by Captain Joseph Ingraham of the *Hope* are the most detailed. The incident also gave rise to a poetic effort, evidently by some person who was present, entitled "Bold Northwestman". One verse from this ballad will suffice:

"Then with what few fire arms we had we rushed on deck amain,
And by our being resolute, our quarter deck we gain'd;
Soon as we gained our arms chest such slaughter then made we,
That in less than ten minutes our ship of them was free."

Kendrick's Land Deals — Apparently the captain of the *Lady Washington,* on his return to the North Pacific Coast from China in 1791, was as much interested in acquiring land as he was in buying sea otter pelts. He made at least five purchases of extensive tracts of the country. He had the native chiefs of the district sign formal deeds. These were later the basis of an appeal by his relatives to the United States Government for recognition as owners of the property. One such legal instrument bears the name of Maquinna of Nootka Sound and several of his subordinate chiefs. It sets forth that for ten muskets Kendrick bought the "harbor in the said Nootka-sound, called Chastacktoos . . . with all the land, rivers, creeks, harbors, islands, etc., within nine miles North, East, West and South of said harbor, with all the produce of both sea and land thereto. . . ."

Chapter Three

Schooner Resolution — Materials for the construction of a tender to the *Jefferson* were brought from Boston in the hold of that vessel. They were unloaded at Resolution Bay, Christina Island of the Marquesas Group. The original intention was to build a schooner of twenty tons, but the plan was enlarged to provide for a ninety-ton craft. She was given the name of the bay in which she was launched and delighted her master, Burling, by her excellent speed and sailing qualities. She accompanied the *Jefferson* to the American Coast and proved her worth in a year of trading operations. In the summer of 1794 she was to rendezvous with the *Jefferson* off the Queen Charlottes, but failed to keep the appointment. Captain Roberts of the *Jefferson* was convinced that she had gone down in a great storm that raged about the time appointed for the meeting.

Burling's Brother — The brother of the murdered master of the *Resolution* was an officer of the Boston vessel *Eliza*. He was informed by a native at Kaigani, Dall Island, that his brother and Solomon Kendrick, son of Captain John Kendrick, had been slain by Scatseye, Cumshewa's brother. The Indian in disclosing the fate of the men had incited him to avenge their deaths by killing Scatseye, whom he hated. When, after the ruse of disguising the nationality of the *Eliza,* Burling captured Scatseye he did not kill him with his own hands, but carried him to Kaigani and turned him over to his enemy. Thus he assured himself that punishment would be meted out to the treacherous chief and rewarded his informant.

Relic of the Resolution — In 1944 logging operations at Cumshewa Inlet unearthed a small cannon which was later presented to the B.C. Archives. Bob Swanson, "the poet laureate of the loggers", was present when the weapon was found. He questioned old Indians about it and was told that it was from a Boston schooner that had been taken by the Indians more than a century ago. He was informed that larger guns were believed to be buried in the vicinity.

The Log of the Ruby — The well kept log of this British vessel is one of the prized possessions of the B.C. Provincial Archives. Captain Bishop was so impressed with the story told to him by Captain Thomas Burnett, of the scow *Mercury,* that he covered pages with

117

a recital of the facts concerning the massacre of the officers and men of the *Resolution* and the adventures of the lone survivor. It is probable that Bears, the former Haida slave, dictated many of the details set down by Bishop.

Chapter Four:
John Rodgers Jewitt — The hero of this story was born in Lincolnshire, England in 1783. He obtained a fair education in his youth, it being the hope of his parents that he would become a physician. He, however, had no liking for the profession of medicine so learned the trade of his father who was a blacksmith. The *Boston* visited England prior to starting on the long voyage to the American West Coast and the Jewitts were employed to effect some ironwork repairs. Captain Salter took a liking to the youth, who in addition to his capabilities as a worker in iron, was a good natured and pleasant individual, and induced his father to permit him to join the company of the *Boston.* After his release from captivity John took up residence in New England where he married. Several children were born to the Jewitts before John's death at the early age of thirty-seven at Hartford, Connecticut, in 1821.

Jewitt's Two Books — Before the *Boston* was destroyed by fire, Jewitt managed to secure a blank book, the pages of which he later filled with notes of the life of himself and Thompson among the Nootkans, using ink made from berry juices and charcoal. Upon reaching Boston in 1807 he had this unvarnished tale published. Copies of the book, which may be referred to as the "Journal" are rare. Eight years later he revised it in collaboration with Richard Alsop, an experienced writer, elaborating and "polishing" the text. This work, which may be called the "Narrative," was an instant success. Greater dependence has been placed upon the Journal and on the statement given to the press by Captain Hill of the *Lydia,* in the compilation of the brief review of Jewitt's adventures published in the present book.

Chapter Five:
Hughes' Fatal Touch — The Governor and Committee of the Hudson's Bay Company have generously permitted use to be made of information contained in official reports to the Company concerning the slaying of Hughes and the others at Fort St. John. Francis Heron, in his "Statement of Circumstances . . ." gives an excuse that Indians advanced for the slaughter: "On the 1st of Novr. Mr. Hughes had tried to engage from among the Indians at this place one from among all of them, to act as guide to some caches of provisions, but that all of them, except one young man had refused to go, upon this young man's consenting to guide people as was required, Mr. Hughes, it is said taped (sic) him on the shoulder, saying he should pay him well for his ready compliance. The Indian young man shortly after retired to his tent, apparently in good health, but in a few hours, suddenly took ill, and died that night, which the Indians attributed

118

to Mr. Hughes having thrown some destructive medicine upon him when he tap(p)ed him on the shoulder, and under this plea, determined, next day to assassinate Mr. Hughes himself, which was no difficult matter to accomplish."

The absurdity of this Indian attempt to justify the murders is evidenced by the attempt made to shoot the men in the canoes going up the river before Mr. Hughes spoke to the Indians about guides to the caches.

Chapter Six:
Fort George Murders — First word of the tragedy at Fort George was received at the district headquarters at Fort St. James from John McDonnell, officer in charge at Fraser Lake. He wrote: "On the 8th Instant an Indian arrived from Fort George, who relates, that during the absence of Mr. Yale . . . both his men were murdered in the House & part of the Property carried off, my informant has seen both the Bodies & says that when Mr. Yale reached the Fort, the Dogs had devoured the Corpse of the Deceased Du Plante . . ."

Douglas Taken by Kwah — Numerous stories have been written about the capture of Fort St. James. After considering them all it was decided that the one most likely to approximate the actual facts was that told by John Tod in his unpublished reminiscences, a transcript of which is in the B.C. Provincial Archives. Tod was stationed in New Caledonia at the time and would have better facilities for obtaining the facts than would more modern writers.

Fraser Lake Incident — John McDonnell, clerk in charge at Fort Fraser, in a letter to Chief Factor Connolly, dated November 7, 1828, gave an account of what took place: "On his way thither Mr. Douglas had a narrow escape at the Village. He had no sooner arrived there, than the Thle ut kek & Sycur Indians rushed towards him all armed with the avowed intention of killing him. He & his men, however, kept them at bay until Yazecho and the Indians of this village who all interposed to prevent them, had succeeded. When he had crossed the River, seeing that they intended to follow him, he fortunately resolved to wait for them & face them in the plain. Where a very tumultuous scene ensued (there were at the time at least one hundred and twenty men at the Village) The particulars of which himself is best able to inform you of. His conduct on the Occasion has certainly impressed the minds of the Natives with a higher opinion of the Whites than previously entertained. Had he not waited for them in the plain, they would have followed him to the Fort, and that in the enraged state they were in would inevitably have led to bloodshed."

Chapter Seven:
First Report of Trouble — Dr. William Fraser Tolmie, then stationed at Nisqually, wrote in his diary of the receipt of startling news from Fort McLoughlin. Under date of November 25, 1833, he set

Chief Factor John Tod, above, whose diaries in the Provincial Archives are the basis for the account on the life of James Douglas at Fort St. James.
At right, above, is Governor Richard Blanshard whose short term in 1850 as the first governor of Vancouver's Island was an unhappy one.
Below is the Songhees Indian Reserve at Victoria in 1868. The Songhees developed into staunch allies of the HBC, once even taking up arms to defend Fort Victoria from a threatened attack by Indians from Cape Flattery.

down: "There are bad news from Millbank; a man who had been repeatedly thrashed by Mr. Manson deserted & went among the Indians. Mr. Manson failing by other means to bring him back, seized a chief & kept him as a prisoner, the Indians surrounding the fort by night seized a man who had gone out for water & said they would keep him until their chief was released. A cannon was then fired which killed five and wounded 3 savages — afterwards an exchange of prisoners took place but the deserter had not appeared on the 15 Novr; . . . Mr. M. has refused to pay for those killed until the runaway is restored. After the affray work was suspended at the fort & those who carried in water were guarded by an armed party at the gallery. Peace was made before the *Lama* sailed but in what manner we have not learnt."

Chapter Eight:

Songhees Indians — In the years that followed the attack on Fort Victoria there were difficulties with the natives, but usually the cause of any disturbance lay with strangers who were visiting the big village across the harbor. The Songhees became very friendly with their white neighbors and, indeed, extended a sort of protectorate over the place and on one occasion, it is reported, took up arms to defend the fort when it was rumored that a band from Cape Flattery was coming to take it. They were jealous of Finlayson's favor, and on one or two occasions he had to discipline them for seeking to set up a monopoly of trade by frightening other Indians, who came to barter their furs, with threats of attacking them if they did not go home. In 1848 Finlayson thought it would be a useful lesson to show the Songhees how the white men fought. He induced Captain Courtenay of H.M.S. *Constance* to land several hundred sailors and marines for the purpose of staging a sham battle. When the affair concluded, the captain asked one chief what he thought of the demonstration. "That way white man fight?" the Indian demanded. "Yes," was the reply. "Huh", grunted the old warrior, "white man fool: Indian get behind tree or rock to shoot."

Chapter Nine:

Governor Richard Blanshard — The sick and discouraged first executive officer of Vancouver's Island was very bitter against the Hudson's Bay Company and Chief Factor James Douglas. He bombarded the Colonial Office with complaints about them. No rumor was too improbable or vicious for him to reject if it discredited the company or its chief official at Victoria. He reported to London a baseless tale to the effect that the Company's representatives at Fort Rupert had instigated the murders there by offering a "dead or alive" reward for the apprehension of the deserters.

Dr. J.S. Helmcken, who was located at the coal mining establishment at the time, in his memoirs criticises Blanshard for purveying such a story and attributes his resignation the following year to his having done so, rather than to ill health. There is no doubt that Blanshard had reason for disappointment. Conditions in the Colony were entirely different from those he had been led to believe existed. He had no salary or expense account from the Crown. He anticipated that the revenues from an "estate" to be granted to him would be sufficient, but on his arrival discovered that the lands were not to be his personally and that they were uncleared and unoccupied. Douglas, on the other hand, regarded Blanshard as an interloper who had been appointed to the position that had been promised to him. It was poor solace to Douglas to know that he drew the salary and that Blanshard had the honor.

Chapter Ten:
The Indian Murderers — It is extraordinary — and regrettable — that there is not more information available in respect to the Indians who were given the tragic distinction of being the first individuals to be formally tried by jury in the Colony of Vancouver's Island. The name of the Cowichan, according to an article written in 1899 by Mackay, was Squeis or Sque-sa (Mackay gave both spellings). The young Nanaimo brave was known as Siam-a-sit. He was the son of Tche-whe-tum. Mackay describes the final act in the drama in the following words: "The (Nanaimo) Indian was discovered, knocked down and handcuffed in an instant, and the next morning he and the young Cowichan, Squeis, who had been arrested at Cowichan by the party on their way up to Nanaimo were tried for murder on the quarterdeck of the steamer *Beaver,* found guilty and executed, those events happened between the hours of 10 a.m. and 3 p.m. on a frosty day in January 1853".

Chapter Eleven:
Conflicting Casualty Reports — It is impossible to accurately determine the number of persons killed in the fighting on the Fraser. The total of white men who perished is given all the way from four or five to more than one hundred. The variation in Indian losses is equally as great. According to Ned Stout there were many white victims to the fury of the natives. He used to relate how a number of Cornish miners were killed in the Little Canyon, and of a number of Frenchmen who died in a fight near Boston Bar, while there were many individuals who were surprised singly or in smaller parties and slaughtered. In addition to these deaths were the score of his own companions in the running fight from Nicomen to China Bar. Owing to the fact that there was no organized government in existence on the Mainland at the time there is a lack of official records, while the shifting character of the population in the summer of 1858 made it difficult to check up on missing men.

Chapter Twelve:
Lived In Danger — The settlers on Saltspring Island were in constant fear of being made the innocent victims of inter-tribal warfare. The frequent killings that took place on and about the island kept

them in a state of alarm. Following the massacre at Ganges they met at Lineker's house and drafted a request to Governor Douglas for protection.

In the letter to the Governor, Lineker wrote: "The Indians have all left here, probably anticipating an attack. In such an event we should be anything but safe, especially should they in any way molest the settlers. We number here twenty-six men scattered over about two miles square. Considering their defenceless position the settlers trust that Your Excellency will deem it expedient to afford them such protection as you in your wisdom may deem necessary."

Chapter Thirteen:

Aid to Civil Power — Captain Robson in his official report to Admiral Sir Thomas Maitland of the fight with the Haidas gave his reason for proceeding to follow them north of Nanaimo. His instructions had been to investigate what they had been doing on Admiral (Saltspring) Island and at Nanaimo. "Bearing in mind," he said, "that the Indian Savage fully appreciates prompt retributive justice, I believed I should be best ensuring the safety, not only of the Settlers but of the Public at large by assisting the Civil Authorities which were powerless against such desperate and overwhelming numbers, and therefore most willingly acceded to the annexed request from Mr. Franklyn. . . ."

Governor Douglas strongly endorsed Robson's actions, writing on the margin of Admiral Maitland's letter: "I entirely approve of Captain Robson's proceedings in regard to the Hyder Indians who fired upon and insulted her Majestys Flag — and set the civil authorities of the Colony at defiance — The punishment inflicted upon them was the result of their own rashness and was merited and necessary."

Chapter Fourteen:

Final Act — Notes of Chief Justice Cameron, entered in record of assizes, June 17, and after, 1863: *"Regina vs Whan-uck:* Prisoner was convicted of assisting Pollak in killing of Frederick Marks and Mrs. Caroline Harvey, on Kulman (or Saturna) Island. Evidence of Nuchuss, an Indian woman, was to effect that Pollak, since shot, killed Marks, while the accused stabbed Mrs. Harvey. Both bodies were weighted with stones and sunk. — Verdict, Guilty; sentenced to hang, July 4.

"Regina vs Quah-ah-ilton, She-nall-ou-ouck, Ot-chee-wun: Evidence of Horace Smith, superintendent of police, told of fight in Village Bay, Kuper Island, when sailor, Gliddon was killed. All found guilty — sentenced to hang, July 4."

Civil Force — Soon after taking office in 1851 Governor Douglas must have organized the "Voltigeurs," a company of half-breed scouts, as mention is made of them in the "Cowichan campaign" of 1852 when the murderers of Peter Brown were sought. They were also credited with having done useful work at Cowichan in 1856 and evidently distinguished themselves in the hunt for Ot-chee-wun and his band.

Chapter Fifteen:
Fatal Negligence — Police Inspector Chartres Brew in his report upon the Bute Inlet massacre commented, in part: "It is difficult to understand how men could have such blind confidence in fickle savages as those murdered men had. There was in camp a store of all things most coveted by Indians; clothes, powder, balls, sugar, flour, meat &c., and all the time it was known that the Indians were little removed from a state of starvation, yet not the slightest effort was made to obtain the goodwill of the Indians or to guard against their enmity . . . The Indians have, I believe, been most injudiciously treated. If a sound discretion had been exercised towards them I believe this outrage would not have been perpetrated."

Canoes were as vital to the Indians of the Northwest Coast as horses were to the Indians on the Plains. As the photos on these two pages indicate, canoes varied in size. The one at left is at Nootka Sound, those above at Nanaimo in 1868 and the big, elaborately carved one at right is taking guests to a wedding. A costumed dancer stands at the bow.

Mountain Fighting — In his despatch to the Colonial Office Governor Seymour gave a descriptive account of the difficulties and obstacles that confronted the Cariboo Volunteers in their pursuit of the rebels towards the head of Bute Inlet: ". . . the Northern Volunteers marched towards the Bute Inlet mountains without much knowledge of the reception they would meet with. It was one of deadly hostility. The Indians kept close to them, unseen generally, but ever present scouts dogged the white man's steps. Indians on horseback kept just beyond rifle range. Endless perplexing trails, running in circles, or ending in water, were prepared for their special embarrassment. The trees about the Indian camps had figures of white men cut on them, which had been used as targets for musket practice. One chief carried his boldness to the point of coming to warm himself at the camp fire before Mr. Cox had gone 200 yards off. Shots were repeatedly exchanged with what effect on the enemy we know not, but Mr. McLean the 2nd in command received a bullet

through the heart. On the day which he fell Mr. Cox turned back and retreated his steps towards Benshee."

Chapter Sixteen:
Denman's Disappointment — Such was the indignation of the Admiral at the refusal of Mr. Justice Cameron to hear Indian witnesses that his clerk appeared to have difficulty in putting Denman's letter of protest to Governor Kennedy into polite language. The Admiral believed that the action of the court would be misinterpreted by the Indians and endanger white traders. It would appear from subsequent events on the coast that there was some justification for this fear. It is hard to understand the reason for Judge Cameron's ruling, as the previous year he had hanged an Indian upon the testimony of another native.

Chapter Seventeen:
Captain Turnour's Statement — In his report to Governor Kennedy, the captain said: ". . . in consequence of the Indians at Fort Rupert having threatened my men, I burnt the Ranch to the ground, destroyed about one Hundred Canoes and a quantity of Spirit. I have brought a Chief called Jim who was foremost in endeavouring to create a disturbance, and a few other prisoners that I deemed it necessary to remove for the present." Despite the threats of Chief Jim the punishment inflicted on the tribe was out of proportion to the offence.

Chapter Eighteen:
Chief Isadore's Position — There is no doubt that Chief Isadore restrained his people from going to more dangerous lengths in defiance of the law. He met the settlers and assured them that he did not want trouble and it was the settlers, by a majority vote, who asked the provincial police to leave the district.

In a report made by the white men attending this meeting to Magistrate Vowell and published in the *Victoria Times,* March 27, 1887, this fact is acknowledged: "The question was then put amongst the white people as to whether the gentlemen named should, or should not leave the country, and it was decided by the majority that in the interest of peace, they should be asked to do so for the present."

In the same report the impossible situation created by the action of Isadore and his men was tersely indicated: ". . . we would beg to point out for all practical purposes the white law amongst the Indians is inoperative, for should the constable attempt an arrest for a serious offence, the offender is either screened from justice or released by main force; the settlers being powerless to assist the authorities in maintaining the law."

Isadore asked that Indian Commissioner Dr. I.W. Powell be sent to the district. When Powell, Herchmer and Vowell, as a commission, visited the Kootenays shortly after this request, the whole trouble was settled.

More *Heritage House* Books on Western Canada

OUTLAWS AND LAWMEN OF WESTERN CANADA — Volume One: Some of Western Canada's dramatic crimes. Includes Alberta Indian Swift Runner, who ate his mother, brother, wife and six children; Saskatchewan's first stagecoach holdup; the 1880 death on duty of Manitoba's pioneer police chief; British Columbia's "Phantoms of the Rangeland," and many others. 128 pages, photos, maps. **$6.95**

OUTLAWS AND LAWMEN OF WESTERN CANADA — Volume Two: More of Western Canada's dramatic crimes. There is Jess Williams, in 1884 the first man hanged in Calgary; Saskatchewan's Almighty Voice whose murder of a policeman in 1895 caused six other deaths; B.C.'s Henry Wagner who in 1912 was hanged so quickly that he set a world record; and many others. 128 pages, photos, maps. **$6.95**

TRAGEDIES OF THE CROWSNEST PASS: In Canada no place equals the tragedies of the Crowsnest Pass on the Alberta-B.C. border. At Hillcrest a mine explosion killed 189 out of 235 men; at Frank a mountain collapsed, killing upwards of 100 residents; and at Fernie a mine explosion killed 128 men. 96 pages. **$5.95**

OKANAGAN VALLEY: This guide reveals the many wonders of a Valley of beaches and blossoms; wineries and history; sunshine and — perhaps — a genial Okanagan Lake resident called Ogopogo. 128 pages. **$7.95**

TALES OF CONFLICT: Indian-White Battles and Massacres in Pioneer B.C.: Contrary to popular belief, B.C. was not settled peacefully. Hundreds of whites and Indians died in murders and massacres from Vancouver Island to the Fraser Canyon, East Kootenay to the Chilcotin. 128 pages. **$7.95**

STAGECOACH AND STERNWHEEL DAYS IN THE CARIBOO AND CENTRAL B.C.: For fifty years from 1863 when the first stagecoach rumbled northward from Yale until 1921 when the sternwheeler *Quesnel* was destroyed in Fort George Canyon, colorful stagecoaches and sternwheelers served Central B.C. 96 pages. **$5.95**

SLUMACH'S GOLD — In Search of a Legend: Do the Coast Mountains some 40 miles northwest of Vancouver guard gold worth upwards of $100 million? **$3.95**

INCREDIBLE ROGERS PASS: In this 55-mile section of the Trans-Canada Highway, over 200 men died keeping the CPR's main line open. Today snowsheds and artillery protect motorists from snowfall which can exceed 700 inches a year. **$3.95**

THE HOPE SLIDE — Disaster in the Dark: In the darkness 100 million tons of rock buried B.C.'s Southern Trans-Provincial Highway over 100 feet deep, engulfing motorists already trapped by a snow slide. **$3.95**

126 STOPS OF INTEREST IN BEAUTIFUL BRITISH COLUMBIA: Describes the Stop-of-Interest signs which honor pioneers, identify flora and fauna, points of historical interest and similar features along B.C.'s highways. 130 pages. **$4.95**

THE OVERLANDERS OF 1862: From Fort Garry the 150 gold seekers headed west in ox-carts for the goldfields of Cariboo, 1,500 wilderness miles away. Months later they arrived — speed 12 miles a day, five dead, the rest lucky to survive. **$3.95**

Bill Miner . . . STAGECOACH AND TRAIN ROBBER: The famous Pinkerton Detective Agency called him ". . . the master criminal of the American West." In a lifetime of crime he stole some $250,000, including $7,000 during Canada's first train holdup in B.C. in 1904 — and escaped from every jail he was in. **$4.95**

HANGING IN CANADA . . . Concise History of a Controversial Topic: Once over 200 offences carried the death penalty. Ontario's first hanging was for burglary; in 1803 a thirteen-year-old boy was hanged in Montreal for stealing a cow. **$3.95**

THE RIEL REBELLION — 1885: In 1870 Riel won the Metis representative government when the province of Manitoba was founded. In 1884-85 he again led Metis in their fight for fair treatment. The results were tragic, with death to many — including Riel. 96 pages. **$5.95**

FROG LAKE MASSACRE: On April 17, 1885, came a message from what is today Alberta: "There's been a massacre at Frog Lake. All the white men have been murdered and their wives taken prisoner by Big Bear's Plains Crees." This book describes the massacre, pursuit of Big Bear, and the experiences of nearly fifty prisoners living under daily threat of execution. **$5.95**

CHUCKWAGON RACING — Calgary Stampede's Half Mile of Hell: Four wagons behind sixteen galloping horses chased by sixteen outriders makes chuckwagon racing one of the world's most dangerous sports. Born at the Calgary Stampede in 1923, its heritage is the rangeland of the Canadian West. **$4.95**

The Death of ALBERT JOHNSON . . . Mad Trapper of Rat River: One intriguing mystery remains in this saga of pursuit and shoot-out in the numbing cold of Canada's Arctic over half a century ago — WHO WAS ALBERT JOHNSON? **$3.95**

Gabriel Dumont . . . Jerry Potts — CANADIAN PLAINSMEN: Had Dumont and Potts lived in the U.S., they would be as well known as Davy Crockett and Daniel Boone, frontiersmen whom Dumont and Potts equalled in skill and courage. **$3.95**

BANFF — PARK OF ALL SEASONS: A 15-square-mile reserve around a Rocky Mountain hotspring in 1885 developed into Banff National Park. Today Banff covers over 3,500 square miles and hosts over three million visitors a year. **$2.95**

MAJESTIC JASPER: Mt. Edith Cavell, Miette Hot Springs and Maligne Lake; wildlife from moose to mountain sheep; and year-round activities from skiing to hiking, attract two million people yearly to this largest of Western National Parks. **$2.95**

WATERTON NATIONAL PARK: The Indians knew it as "Land of the Shining Mountains," a unique area in southwestern Alberta where prairie meets the mountains and nature sculpted lakes and valleys against a snow-peaked background. **$2.95**

MAGNIFICENT YELLOWHEAD HIGHWAY — Volume One: From Portage la Prairie to the Pacific Ocean, the Yellowhead is a panorama of prairie, plains and mountains. This volume describes 750 miles from Portage to Edmonton. **$2.95**

MAGNIFICENT YELLOWHEAD HIGHWAY — Volume Two: From Edmonton 504 miles through Jasper National Park to the sagebrush country of B.C. **$2.95**

MAGNIFICENT YELLOWHEAD HIGHWAY — Volume Three: From Mount Robson, the Rockies highest peak, westward 628 miles through some of North America's most scenic sport fishing country to tidewater at Prince Rupert. **$2.95**

STOPS OF INTEREST IN SOUTHERN ALBERTA: Along Alberta's highways are over 100 historical markers that describe unique geographical features, events of historical significance and honor pioneers. Here are those in southern Alberta. **$3.95**

STOPS OF INTEREST IN CENTRAL AND NORTHERN ALBERTA: Descriptions of historical markers along highways in Central and Northern Alberta. **$3.95**

THE CYPRESS HILLS OF ALBERTA-SASKATCHEWAN: Twenty miles wide, 200 miles long, nearly 5,000 feet high, they are a unique landform — ranking with the Grand Canyon and the desert of Western America. **$3.95**

GHOST TOWNS OF SOUTHERN ALBERTA — Volume One: Silver City, Bankhead, Mitford, Brant, Cleverville and other communities were once home to thousands. Today they survive only in photos, newspapers and memories. **$3.95**

GHOST TOWNS OF MANITOBA: During the surge of settlement scores of Manitoba towns were born. Scores also died. Some of them were Manitoba City, Bannerman, Odanah, Asessippi, Millwood, Ewart, Millford, Grand Valley, Dropmore and Hecla. 31 chapters, over 100 photos. 160 pages. **$9.95**

Available at bookstores and other outlets throughout B.C., Alberta, Saskatchewan and Manitoba. If not available order direct from Heritage House Publishing Company, Box 1228, Station A, Surrey, B.C. V3S 2B3. Payment can be by cheque or money order. Books are shipped postpaid.